GREAT INVENTIONS

Navigational Aids

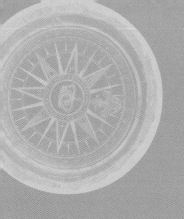

GREAT INVENTIONS

Navigational Aids

LINDA WILLIAMS

mc **Marshall Cavendish**
Benchmark

New York

Marshall Cavendish Benchmark
99 White Plains Road
Tarrytown, NY 10591-9001
www.marshallcavendish.us

Library of Congress Cataloging-in-Publication Data

Williams, Linda D.
Navigational aids / Linda Williams.
p. cm. — (Great inventions)
Summary: "An examination of the origins, history, development, and impact
of the various navigational aids humans have used through the
centuries"—Provided by publisher.
Includes bibliographical references and index.
ISBN-13: 978-0-7614-2599-1
1. Aids to navigation—Juvenile literature. I. Title. II. Series.

VK381.W55 2007
387.1'55—dc22
2006028959

Series design by Sonia Chaghatzbanian

Photo research by Candlepants Incorporated

Cover photo: Thom Lang/Corbis

The photographs in this book are used by permission and through the courtesy of: *Corbis:*
Sanford/Agliolo, 2; Schultheiss Productions/zefa, 8; Michael Freeman, 23; Sandro Vannini, 36;
Stockbyte, 50; Stefano Bianchetti, 58, 79; Maps.com, 60-61; Jeff Zaruba, 70; Image 100, 72;
Matthias Kulka/zefa, 74; Hulton-Deutsch Collection, 75; Charles O'Rear, 89; Onne van der Wal, 90;
Matthias Kulka, 92; Steve Kaufman, 96; Hein van den Heuvel/zefa, 98; ESA/Handout/epa, 101; Ilya
Naymushin, 106; Paul A. Souders, 109; Nation Wong/zefa, 110; 80-81. *The Bridgeman Art Library:*
©Bibliotheque Nationale, Paris, France, 11; ©Private Collection, 32, 27; ©Musee National de la
Renaissance, Ecouen, France/ Giraudon, 41; ©Museu Nacional de Arte Antigua, Lisbon, Portugal,
52; ©Private Collection/ Archives Charmet, 76. *Art Resource, NY:* Werner Forman, 13; HIP, 18;
Snark, 26; Erich Lessing, 64. *Art Archive:* Private Collection/Dagli Orti, 14; Bibliotheque des Arts
Decoratifs Paris/Dagli Orti, 16; Bibliotheque Nationale Paris, 20. *The Image Works:* Oxford Science
Library/Heritage-Images, 24; SSPL, 34, 45, 47, 29, 31; Science Museum/SSPL, 42; Topham, 55,
66; The British Library/Topham-HIP, 68. *Photo Researchers Inc.:* Gary Hincks, 39. *Getty Images:*
Hulton Archive, 48; 62; Aurora, 83; Chris Beeson/Allsport, 86; Eric Estrade/AFP, 88; Catrina
Genovese, 95; Carsten Peter/National Geographic, 103; ESA, 105.

Printed in Malaysia
1 3 5 6 4 2

CONTENTS

Navigational Aids

HAVE YOU EVER BEEN LOST? A MAP IS A SIMPLE NAVIGATIONAL AID THAT IS OFTEN TAKEN FOR GRANTED. IMAGINE THE DIFFICULTY OF GETTING TO A NEW DESTINATION WITHOUT THE USE OF ONE—OR ITS DIGITAL, ONLINE EQUIVALENT.

ONE

Ancient Mariners

Have you ever been lost? You thought you knew where you were and then found yourself turned around. All the houses looked the same, yet the streets were strangely familiar. Were you supposed to turn left or right at the fork in the road? It happens to everyone. Some of us stop and ask for directions; some keep searching for the right path.

Now, what if you were on the ocean, with no landmarks around, just water everywhere and the sun, moon, and stars as your only guides. How would you know where you were going? How would you find your way?

You would need to find a workable path from one place to another or *navigate.* The word comes from the Latin root word *navis,* meaning "ship," and *agere,* meaning "to move or direct."

Navigation has often been challenging and problematic since humans built the first ships and attempted long sea voyages across the ocean. No one really knows when humans first went to sea. Early on, sailors kept their boats close to shore and within sight of land. They attempted short one- or two-day trips along the coast or to a nearby island or landmass. Eventually growing bolder, sailors extended their voyages to several weeks or months. Items were taken along to exchange for goods that people did not have or could not get in their own area. To find their way both to and from increasingly distant destinations, sailors had to observe the direction of the currents and the wind, the color of the water, and the landmarks onshore. On repeat voyages, navigators relied on previous experience and tapped the knowledge and familiarity they had gained of ocean waters and currents, the wind, and the geographic features of particular coastal areas.

Sailors came to use a variety of devices and systems to help them navigate the waters, assess or read their position, and chart their increasingly longer voyages. As science has advanced and knowledge of the world has grown, sailors have adapted and applied ever-new technologies to assist them in navigating the world's unpredictable oceans and seas.

How Deep Is the Water?

Not knowing the exact depth of the water beneath a ship was a major worry for early sailors. The bottom of the ship could be damaged if it scraped against the seafloor or rocks hidden in the shallows. Not knowing what lay below made it difficult to plot a safe course through unfamiliar channels and into protected harbors. If a sailor was not careful, he could run the ship aground. To determine the depth of the water, ancient seamen used one of the oldest marine instruments—a sounding rod. This long pole was lowered into the water to find the sea bottom. Ancient sailors also used a similar instrument, a sounding weight.

A sounding weight is a tear-shaped object usually made of lead. One end has a loop so the weight can be tied to a long line. To check the water's depth, a sailor dropped the sounding weight into the water and noted the length of rope when the weight hit bottom and stopped running over the side of the boat. The sounding weight was critical to aiding navigation of oceans and rivers from the sixth century BCE until modern times.

A sounding weight could have a layer of soft tallow at the base, an addition that allowed a sample to be brought up from the bottom. Often after taking different samples of mud, sand, sea plants, and small sea creatures, knowledgeable ship captains could recognize the features characteristic of a particular locale. Mud, for example, showed that they

THIS ILLUSTRATION SHOWS FOURTEENTH-CENTURY SAILORS USING A MARINER'S ASTROLABE, AN EARLY NAVIGATIONAL AID, IN THE INDIAN OCEAN. AT THE TIME, A SUCCESSFUL JOURNEY TYPICALLY INVOLVED AS MUCH GUESSWORK AND LUCK AS IT DID SKILL. SIMPLE DETERMINATIONS, SUCH AS FINDING THE DEPTH OF THE WATER AT A SPECIFIC POINT, PROVED CHALLENGING.

were near the mouth of a river. Such an indicator, as well as a captain's familiarity with local geography, currents, and winds, helped him direct the ship.

The Ancient Egyptians

The Egyptians relied on their great technological skill to build ships for use on the Nile River and the Mediterranean and Red Seas. Egyptian traders reached the island of Crete in the Mediterranean Sea as long ago as 2500 BCE. A range of vessels was created. The river-going craft could be simple papyrus rafts but sturdier wooden ships were built for the seas. Navigation and nautical imagery soon became recurring elements in ancient Egyptian art. Numerous paintings portray scenes of ship-building and of boats transporting goods and carrying passengers. Scale models of boats, representations intended to ferry esteemed pharaohs into the underworld, have been found in many tombs.

In 1954 the world's oldest ship was discovered deep within the pyramid of King Cheops (an Egyptian who ruled around 1700 BCE). The full-sized ancient ship, considered one of the world's greatest archaeological finds, was dismantled by its builders into 651 separate parts before being placed in the tomb. These parts were found in thirteen orderly layers within a sealed boat pit made of the limestone used to make the Giza plateau, site of a funerary complex.

Measuring 150 feet (46 meters) long, the ship contained 1,224 individual wooden pieces, including cedar planking and wooden dowels that, when assembled, were held together with ropes and copper connectors. The pieces were marked with individual symbols that, when matched with each other, indicated which parts fit together. Egypt's dry climate had preserved 95 percent of the ship's original timbers, but new ropes were needed. No one knows for sure whether the royal ship of King Cheops was meant for the king's use in the afterlife or as part of the funeral rites performed when his attendants transported his body to the pyramid in Giza. It is possible that the king wanted to have a boat ready and nearby that would enable him to oversee the empire that awaited him in his next life.

The Phoenicians

The Phoenicians were a conquering force renowned for their seamanship and the many colonies they founded along the Mediterranean coast. They were masters of coastal navigation, daring to sail into the Atlantic Ocean. Without modern navigational aids or any accurate instruments for choosing a direction, determining position and direction proved a constant challenge to Phoenician sailors. They, along with the

THE FUNERARY BOAT OF KING CHEOPS MAY HAVE BEEN USED FOR RELIGIOUS FESTIVALS AND CEREMONIAL OCCASIONS DURING THE PHARAOH'S LIFETIME. ORIGINALLY FOUND DISMANTLED IN THE RULER'S TOMB COMPLEX, THE RECONSTRUCTED BOAT OFFERS A RARE GLIMPSE INTO THE BOATBUILDING TECHNIQUES AND NAVIGATIONAL PRACTICES OF THE ANCIENT EGYPTIANS.

THIS NINETEENTH-CENTURY WATERCOLOR PORTRAYS A PHOENICIAN TRADING SHIP, LOADED WITH VALUABLE GOODS, ARRIVING AT A PORT ON THE EASTERN MEDITERRANEAN SEA.

Greeks and Romans, faced the same dangers. In those times—when most seamen had only the vaguest sense of direction—straying from a set course or desired destination was common. Like most ancient navigators, the courage to embark on a journey with unknown results yielded hard-won insight and knowledge. From experience, Phoenician sailors knew the directions of the winds and the main currents of the Mediterranean Sea. Navigators also judged direction by consulting the paths of the sun and the moon and the position of Polaris, the North Star.

The Arabs

Early Arab sailors also navigated by the stars. As an aid, they used a device called a *kamal,* which means "guide" in Arabic. A *kamal* is a flat piece of wood, cut to about the size of a sheet of paper. A string was attached to the middle of the piece of wood. To use the kamal effectively, a point of reference needed to be established. When the ship was anchored at the home port, before a voyage was begun, the navigator would tie a knot in the cord so that, when holding the knot in his teeth and holding the rectangular piece (sometimes called a transom) in front of him with the cord taut, he could see the North Star just along the top of the piece and the horizon line along the bottom edge.

Since the Earth's axis points toward the North Star, the star's position in the sky is relatively fixed. This provided the starting-point measurement. On their journey, Arab navigators could then tie knots at different spots on the string to mark various latitudes along the way. The knot positions corresponding to the altitude recorded at frequently visited ports became reliable indicators of a ship's latitude. Over time, the system became more refined and sophisticated. Navigators developed smaller increments to indicate shorter distances. An *issabah* was one such unit of measurement, subdividing the lengths between the various knots. Meaning "finger" in Arabic, the *issabah* was based on the width of a human finger.

The Vikings

A thousand years ago, the Vikings braved the waters of the Atlantic Ocean and sailed southward and westward from Norway and Sweden. They explored the Mediterranean Sea, North Africa, and the rivers of western Russia and Europe. The Vikings were the first Europeans to

THE VIKINGS' KNOWLEDGE OF NAVIGATION WAS DERIVED MOSTLY FROM TRIAL AND ERROR, HARD-WON INSIGHTS, EXPERIENCE, AND BRAVERY. ONE VIKING NAVIGATOR REPORTEDLY RELEASED BIRDS THROUGHOUT HIS VOYAGE. OBSERVING THE DIRECTIONS IN WHICH THEY FLEW HELPED HIM TO DETERMINE AND CORRECT HIS COURSE.

travel to Iceland, Greenland, and North America. They began to colonize as well as raid other lands. The Vikings were not only good shipbuilders, they were skilled navigators and seamen too.

When the Vikings made raids in England, they brought their knowledge of boatbuilding and sailing with them. Many of these raiders settled in England, married local women, and became integrated into their adopted culture and society. Many Viking words connected with ships and sailing were absorbed into the English language. For example, the

Vikings called the right side of a ship *stjornbordi,* the origin of the word *starboard,* the nautical term for the right side of a ship.

When sailing, the Vikings followed simple navigational rules. They sailed during the daytime within sight of land and used familiar landmarks to guide them to their destination. Unless caught in a storm and blown off course, the Vikings seldom went far from the sight of land. These hardy navigators were familiar with regional winds and knew how to use them to their advantage. The sailors observed the water and the wildlife and learned to recognize where they were by the kinds of seaweed floating on the ocean and seabirds flying overhead. When the Vikings were out of sight of land, they released birds and observed the direction in which they flew. The simple test worked well. If the birds flew back to the ship, land was still a long way away. If the birds did not return, then the Vikings pointed their ships in the same direction the birds had flown and headed toward the land. The Vikings also studied the color of mud samples taken from the seafloor to help figure out their location.

Like all mariners, the Vikings used the sun's position and its path across the sky as aids in finding their own position. At sunrise, they noted the sun's position above the horizon in order to ascertain the basic compass points, starting with the east. From this reading, they could determine north, south, and west and work out their heading or direction. At night, the Vikings navigated by the stars. In particular, they used Polaris to orient themselves.

The Vikings primarily navigated by sighting well-known landmarks. They watched for distinctive land formations, rock colors, and previously identified fjords (narrow inlets with steep cliffs on both sides) and mountain peaks to orient themselves and to identify their position. When sailing familiar routes, they knew how to adjust their course, by watching a certain landmark, to arrive at their desired destination. Typically, however, the Vikings mostly sailed along the coastline, eventually gaining the confidence and ability to reach more distant and ambitious places in Scotland, Ireland, Iceland, Greenland, and North America.

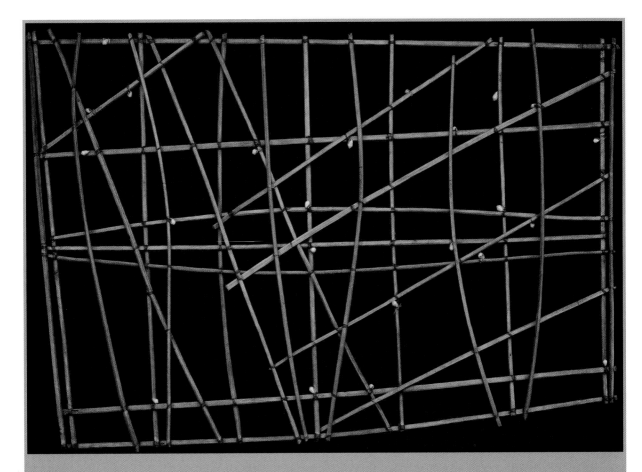

THIS NAVIGATION CHART DATES FROM THE NINETEENTH CENTURY AND REPRESENTS THE TWO CHAINS THAT MAKE UP WHAT ARE TODAY REFERRED TO AS THE MARSHALL ISLANDS. POLYNESIANS MADE CHARTS OF THEIR REGION USING WOVEN PALM FIBERS TO SHOW THE WAVE PATTERNS OF THE PACIFIC OCEAN. IN SOME VERSIONS, SEASHELLS MARKED THE LOCATION OF ISLANDS OR OTHER LANDFALLS.

The Polynesians

For a long time people wondered how the Polynesians traveled among the islands scattered over the vast Pacific Ocean. The distances seemed too great and the islands too small for them to find their destinations and to return home without the use of navigational aids. For these long voyages, the Polynesians sailed by consulting the sun during the day and the stars at night. The place on the horizon where a certain star or constellation rose or set was matched to the location of a particular island. To reach the island, Polynesian sailors pointed their boat toward the guide star. When the guide star rose too high or disappeared below the horizon, a second star following the same path to or from the horizon was chosen. This enabled them to travel between two well-known destinations.

The Polynesians also watched the direction of the ocean waves to get an indication of the direction of the winds. The size and nature of the waves revealed whether the seafarers were in open waters or approaching still-unseen islands. Experienced sailors could spot when the patterns in the water indicated waves that had rebounded from a nearby island. In this way, the Polynesians were able to extend their navigational ability and their area of influence.

In this illustration from the 1580s, a French mariner uses an early navigational device while on steady footing onshore to help determine the ship's position.

Celestial Aids

Humans have traveled to far-flung destinations for thousands of years in search of new lands, religious freedom, better living conditions, or in the hope of making their fortunes. When they could, they traveled during the day and within sight of familiar landmarks. They judged their position by the sun, and at night—when schedules or necessity forced travelers to keep moving—they used the stars as guides. Objects in the sky became directional beacons used by many navigators to set their courses. The ability to navigate by the sun and the stars freed ships from their local waters and coasts. Using the stars, navigators could venture away from shore and into unfamiliar or distant seas, more confident of their chances of arriving safely and accurately at their destinations and then returning home.

When traveling uncharted waters, the presence of the sun, moon, stars, and other celestial objects was often one of the few predictable elements on which voyagers could depend. As aids to navigation, instruments to read the position of these markers and signs were developed. These instruments were probably derived from the *kamal* first used by Arab mariners.

During the Renaissance, celestial navigation, using increasingly accurate instruments and detailed records to find out the positions of the sun and stars, became more and more important. Astronomers put together almanacs listing the altitudes or heights of the sun above the horizon at noon and of the North Star throughout the year in different locations. The altitude of a celestial body was important to a navigator because this reading changed according to the latitude of the ship, the position north or south relative to the equator. If a navigator knew the correct altitude of the sun or a certain star, then he knew his latitude and could direct his course accordingly.

Renaissance navigators typically arrived at a destination by "sailing latitude." To sail latitude, the captain had to know the latitude of the destination before starting out. Once under sail, the ship headed north or south until it reached the latitude matching the desired destination. The ship then turned east or west, depending on the location of the area sought, to its intended goal. Sailing by latitude required the navigator to check the altitude of the sun or the North Star frequently to be sure the ship was staying on course.

The Mariner's Quadrant

A major invention that would transform the world of navigation was the mariner's quadrant, a device that offered a way to measure the altitude of a heavenly body, usually the North Star or the sun. The quadrant first appeared in the 1200s and was in standard navigational use by around 1450.

The mariner's quadrant is a quarter circle of wood or brass with markings along its curved edge. Some quadrants bore markings that indicated the latitudes of different coastal cities such as Lisbon, Portugal, or Tangier, Morocco. Others bore the regular pattern of the 90 individual degrees that make up a quarter circle. A plumb bob, a weight hanging from a string, was suspended from a ring attached at the upper corner of the quarter circle. It provided a vertical point of reference, hanging down and indicating a point on the degree marking along the quadrant's curved edge. On one of the two noncurved edges of the quadrant were two pins with sighting holes. To use the device, one person held it vertically with the curved edge at the bottom. The quadrant was then tilted so that a second person, the viewer, could look through both

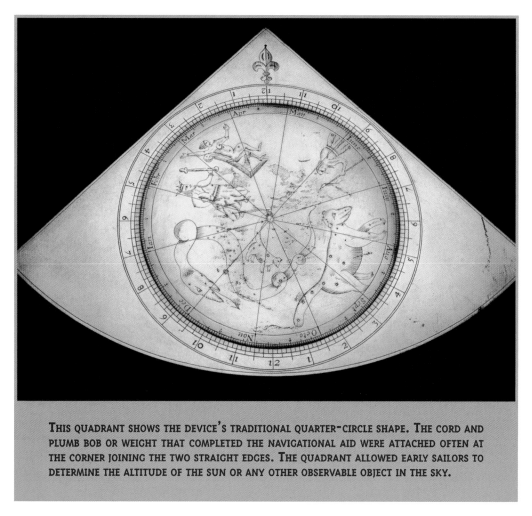

THIS QUADRANT SHOWS THE DEVICE'S TRADITIONAL QUARTER-CIRCLE SHAPE. THE CORD AND PLUMB BOB OR WEIGHT THAT COMPLETED THE NAVIGATIONAL AID WERE ATTACHED OFTEN AT THE CORNER JOINING THE TWO STRAIGHT EDGES. THE QUADRANT ALLOWED EARLY SAILORS TO DETERMINE THE ALTITUDE OF THE SUN OR ANY OTHER OBSERVABLE OBJECT IN THE SKY.

holes to see the sun or the North Star. Where the plumb line crossed the scale or the markings below, the position indicated the altitude of the celestial body. From this information, the navigator had a good idea of his present latitude and whether the ship needed to sail north or south to reach the desired latitude.

One of the quadrant's problems was that two people had to operate it. One person sighted the celestial body, while another person read where the plumb line crossed the scale. This proved tricky onboard a ship rolling in rough seas. Consequently, the quadrant was almost always used at anchor or in port. Even there, it was difficult to keep the

THIS ITALIAN ILLUSTRATION FROM THE 1590S SHOWS A SAILOR, PERCHED HIGH ABOVE THE DECK IN THE SHIP'S CROW'S NEST, USING A QUADRANT TO MEASURE THE CRAFT'S DISTANCE FROM SHORE.

wind from disturbing the plumb line. In addition, to interpret the quadrant's reading, navigators had to have some knowledge of the changing altitude of the sun and the stars at various latitudes or have an almanac listing those figures.

Despite these drawbacks, the quadrant was put to good use by Portuguese mariners and explorers of the fifteenth century. As they sailed south along the African coast, approaching—then crossing—the equator, the North Star could no longer be seen above the horizon and so could not be used as a guide. However, with the quadrant Portuguese seamen in the southern oceans could still read the altitude of the sun at noon and establish their latitude.

Christopher Columbus was familiar with Portuguese navigational practices and knew something about Portuguese sailors' use of the quadrant. Along with a compass, the quadrant was the most advanced navigational instrument he had on his voyages to the New World. But Columbus did not fully understand how to use the quadrant, used it infrequently, and did not get accurate readings of his latitude when he did.

The Mariner's Astrolabe

The mariner's astrolabe, an instrument similar to the mariner's quadrant, was first employed by European sailors in the 1400s and remained in use for about two hundred years. It was a simpler, adapted version of the astrolabe developed in ancient Greece and the Middle East, which astronomers had used for centuries. The astronomer's astrolabe was a flat disk, usually made of brass, with movable rings marked to show the position of the stars and the sun as seen from a specific location and at a specific time or date. The mariner's astrolabe was used to read the altitude of the noonday sun or of a particular star regardless of the user's location on Earth. It lacked the more complex scales that the astronomical device featured. Instead the mariner's version bore a single scale, often marking each of a circle's 360 degrees. The device was comprised of a flat metal circle with an X crossing its cut-out center. Degrees were marked along the circle's outer edge. A two-headed rotatable piece, often called an alidade, had a hole at each end for sighting the sun or a star. The entire dial rotated on a pivot at the center of the mariner's astrolabe.

To sight a star, the astrolabe could be held at eye level, viewed through the openings, and the altitude determined by reading the point indicated by the alidade on the device's degree scale. To use the sun as a point of reference, the astrolabe was hung at arm's length at the side of the body. It was then adjusted so a ray of light passed through the upper

THE MARINER'S ASTROLABE COULD BE ADAPTED DEPENDING ON THE CONDITIONS. IT COULD BE
HELD UP TO THE USER'S EYE OR HELD AT THE SIDE TO CAPTURE AND ALIGN A RAY OF LIGHT.

hole on the alidade and fell precisely on the lower hole. Using either of these methods, as with the quadrant, once altitude had been determined, the navigator could figure out the vessel's latitude.

The Cross-Staff and the Back-Staff

Two additional navigational innovations, the cross-staff and the back-staff, probably resulted from sailors' frustrations with the quadrant. The fact that the staffs could be used by one person and on a moving ship made them the instruments of choice as soon as they appeared.

The cross-staff was invented perhaps as early as the tenth century and was used at first by astronomers. Mariners began to employ the device as a navigational aid in the early sixteenth century. The cross-staff

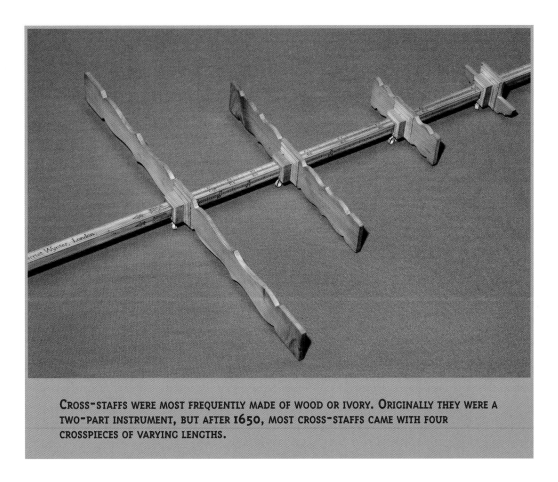

CROSS-STAFFS WERE MOST FREQUENTLY MADE OF WOOD OR IVORY. ORIGINALLY THEY WERE A TWO-PART INSTRUMENT, BUT AFTER 1650, MOST CROSS-STAFFS CAME WITH FOUR CROSSPIECES OF VARYING LENGTHS.

was a length of wood with markings on it. A crossbar, running perpendicular to the main shaft, could be pushed along the length of the main staff to indicate the altitude of the sun or a star. To use a cross-staff, one end of the main piece of wood was held against the cheek so that the eye was exactly positioned to peer down the staff, while the crossbar (like the wooden piece on a *kamal*) was slid forward along the main shaft until it fit into the space between the horizon and the star or the sun. Crossbars of various sizes were available, so a range of altitudes could be read. The different sides of the staff could be marked with various scales as well. The scale would then be converted to degrees of altitude through trigonometry or by consulting a guidebook. To gain an accurate reading, however, the user had to reference two separate points at once with one eye—not an easy task, especially when staring into the sun at the same time. Nevertheless, the device proved popular. Among Dutch mariners, the cross-staff remained in use into the nineteenth century.

The back-staff was created around 1595 by John Davis, an experienced English mariner and scientist. The advantage of this instrument was that it made measuring the altitude of the sun possible without having to look directly at it. Instead, the observer stood with his back to the sun and adjusted the instrument to read a shadow cast by the device. At about the same time, Davis invented a similar instrument, called Davis's quadrant, which also was widely used by English seamen. Davis described the back-staff in *The Seaman's Secrets,* a manual he wrote in 1594 for sailors and not for "scholars to practice upon the shore." His nautical text contained practical navigational advice written in a straightforward way. Most navigational information at that time was available to only a select few members of intellectual societies.

The Sextant

The main problem of these early navigational instruments was that, when sailing, a ship and the people on it were often unsteady. The only reliable way to get accurate sightings was by sending sailors in a small

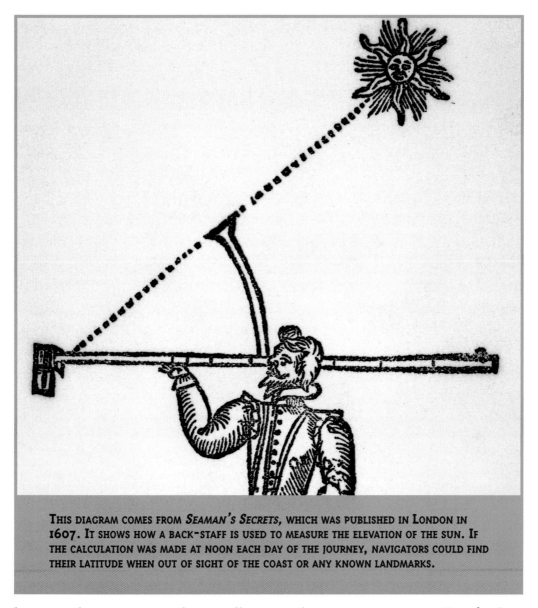

THIS DIAGRAM COMES FROM *SEAMAN'S SECRETS*, WHICH WAS PUBLISHED IN LONDON IN 1607. IT SHOWS HOW A BACK-STAFF IS USED TO MEASURE THE ELEVATION OF THE SUN. IF THE CALCULATION WAS MADE AT NOON EACH DAY OF THE JOURNEY, NAVIGATORS COULD FIND THEIR LATITUDE WHEN OUT OF SIGHT OF THE COAST OR ANY KNOWN LANDMARKS.

boat to shore or a nearby sandbar to take a measurement. But finding such a stable place was not always easy. Life and conditions at sea turned out to be so unpredictable that many captains just hoped that they were on the right course and kept going rather than risk the dangers of stopping. Sometimes this strategy worked; at other times, it landed ill-fated sailors in strange lands with no food and few options.

Necessity brought about the development of an improved instrument that was constructed for use on both land and sea. The efforts of many inventors and navigators led to the development of the sextant. Several people working independently of one another came up with their own designs.

First, Isaac Newton, an English scientist of the seventeenth century, presented his principles of optics to the Royal Society. The design of Newton's sextant—which used a set of double-reflecting mirrors—embodied these notions. It was intended for observing the moon and the stars. Luckily, Newton's fame did not rest on the device's development. He kept on perfecting it until his death and never patented a final design. Plans and specifications for Newton's instrument were discovered among the papers of Royal Society secretary Edmond Halley after his death in 1742.

Robert Hooke, Newton's rival and another Royal Society member, in 1665 described an instrument that was similar to Newton's design except that the mirrors were not in the same double-reflecting arrangement. Hooke's idea was a good one, but it did not work as intended.

Thomas Godfrey, a mathematician from Philadelphia and a colleague of Benjamin Franklin's, made changes to a standard wooden quadrant and designed a double-reflecting quadrant. He asked local ship captains to test the instrument at sea. The results of the trials were favorable, so Godfrey submitted his design to the Royal Society in 1730.

At about the same time, John Hadley, a London instrument maker and mathematician, presented his design for a quadrant to the Royal Society. Hadley, a teenager when Newton first described the possibilities of using a double-reflecting set of mirrors to observe planetary bodies, was curious about the possibilities. If Newton had been alive then—he had died four years earlier—he might have liked Hadley's practical models, which seemed to be an extension of Newton's own designs.

In 1731 the Royal Society published a description of John Hadley's instrument with no mention of Godfrey's work. The design, as recorded

ENGLISH INSTRUMENT MAKER JOHN HADLEY, SHOWN IN A 1728 LITHOGRAPH MADE FROM AN ORIGINAL PAINTING, CONTRIBUTED TO MORE THAN ONE SCIENTIFIC FIELD. HE IMPROVED THE REFLECTOR TELESCOPE IN ADDITION TO INVENTING THE QUADRANT.

in the society's account of Hadley's quadrant, is considered by historians to be the ancestor of the modern double-reflecting sextant.

It is unclear whether the Royal Society snubbed Godfrey's design because members did not approve of it or because he was an American, but at first he did not receive any credit.

John Logan was an acquaintance of not only Godfrey's but of William Penn's, correspondent of the Royal Society and a member of

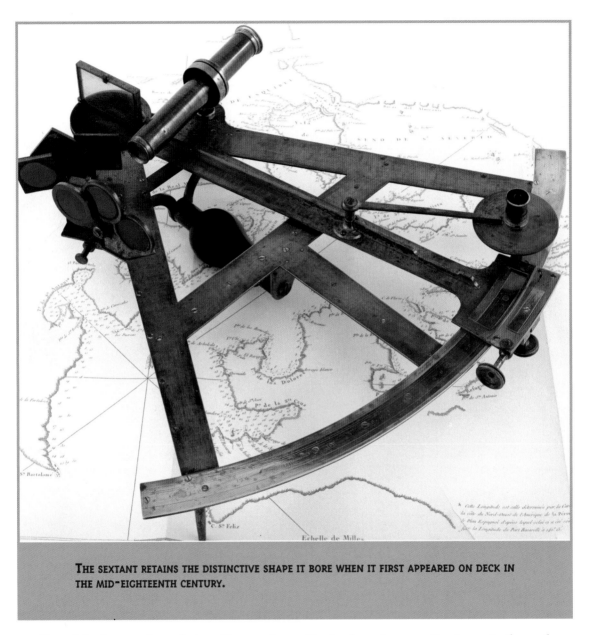

THE SEXTANT RETAINS THE DISTINCTIVE SHAPE IT BORE WHEN IT FIRST APPEARED ON DECK IN THE MID-EIGHTEENTH CENTURY.

Franklin's circle of intellectuals called the Junto. Logan gathered chronological documentation of Godfrey's invention and sent it to the society along with a letter expressing support of Godfrey. Logan also wrote to Hadley and other influential people in London, promoting Godfrey's ingenuity and innovative design. Due in large part to Logan's advocacy, it became apparent that Godfrey and Hadley had developed the reflecting quadrant independently and at the same time.

John Hadley, who was already developing other optical instruments, continued his work. One of Hadley's instruments looked like one-eighth of a circle—an octant—and could measure up to a 90-degree arc. He started production of two types of reflection-based instruments, including a horizon-level glass to help line up a planetary body with the horizon even when the horizon could not be seen. These instruments looked a lot like modern sextants, which have changed shape very little in the past three hundred years. The only differences seen in today's sextants are found in the materials and the larger, better quality mirrors.

A sextant is often kept on hand by modern seamen as a backup in the event their more complex electronic instruments fail or malfunction. If temporarily stranded in the middle of the ocean, sailors who know how to use a sextant can still figure out where they are. Although new technologies have radically altered the nature and methods of navigation today, some of the simple and effective devices of the past can still prove useful.

THE MARINER'S COMPASS FIRST APPEARED IN EUROPE IN THE FOURTEENTH CENTURY. THIS FRENCH-MADE INSTRUMENT DATES TO THE 1770S AND IS REPRESENTATIVE OF THE COMPASSES IN COMMON USE AMONG MEDITERRANEAN SAILORS OF THE TIME.

THREE

Pointing the Way

North, south, east, and west are commonly accepted directions on a map. Most of us have been taught to find our way to a destination by using these directions. But what about early sailors, adrift beneath an overcast sky, with no way of figuring out where they were and in what direction their ship was traveling? The development of the compass added more certainty to journeys undertaken with grave reservations or avoided altogether. Just as the Earth presents navigational challenges, it can also offer amazing solutions. The magnetic field generated by the Earth's core serves as its own form of navigational signal. Experimenters and navigators learned to use and benefit from this invisible guide, overcoming some of the uncertainty and imprecision that early seafarers had faced when plotting their courses.

Clues from the Wind

The movement of the wind, nearly everywhere in the world, follows daily and seasonal patterns. It blows in a steady direction or changes in a predictable way at predictable times of the year. Certain winds have a reputation for being hot or cold, damp or dry, or for bringing fair weather or storms. By the time of Homer, an ancient Greek writer and philosopher who lived about 900 BCE, the Greeks had named the four main directions from which the winds blew. Other Greek philosophers believed there were eight or twelve winds. In Athens, the Tower of the

ALSO KNOWN AS THE HOROLOGION OF ANDRONICUS, NAMED FOR THE MACEDONIAN
ASTRONOMER WHO HAD THE STRUCTURE BUILT, THE TOWER OF THE WINDS WAS ORIGINALLY
TOPPED BY A BRONZE WEATHER VANE AND FEATURED SUNDIALS AND A COMPLEX WATER CLOCK.

Winds, a water clock and observatory built around 100 BCE and still standing to this day, has the figures and the names of eight winds carved in stone around its top. These are north, south, east, and west, along with northeast, northwest, southeast, and southwest. In Greek, these winds were named after various gods.

Mediterranean sailors of later centuries adopted Italian names for each of the main directions from which the wind blew: *tramontana* (north), *ostro* (south), *levante* (east), and *ponente* (west), along with *Greco* (northeast), *maestro* (northwest), *sirocco* (southeast), and *africus* (southwest). On charts, winds were often portrayed by drawings of the gods blowing a gust of wind from one of their eight directions. The directions of the winds were also shown on charts by a pointed star, called a wind rose. Each point represented one of the winds and was labeled with an initial.

One Big Magnet

The huge magnetic field that surrounds the Earth offers another way to find these primary directions. At the center of the Earth is a metal core. The pressure on the core is so great that, despite the extremely high temperatures found there, the metal of the inner core is solid. Surrounding the inner core is an outer layer of molten metal. As the Earth orbits the sun, the Earth's magnetic field is created by the solid inner core, by the movement of the currents in the hot liquid outer core, and by the movement of slower currents within the Earth's mantle—the layer sandwiched between the outer core and the crust. The rotation of the Earth on its axis also contributes by influencing the direction of the hot currents in the outer core.

Scientists believe that Earth's iron-nickel outer core and its ever-moving energy field are converted into electrical charges. Intense heat and chemical reactions increase the power of the electrical charges and contribute to the production of the magnetism. The result of the electrical charges and constant movement of the core is that the Earth is a giant magnet. Invisible lines of magnetic force loop between the North

Pole and the South Pole and extend far beyond the Earth's atmosphere and out into space.

The magnetic poles and the geographic poles are not located in the same place, though. The top and bottom points of the globe are geographically always in the same unchanging positions, but the location of the magnetic poles drifts. At this time, magnetic north moves at a rate of 9 miles (14.5 kilometers) per year. Today it is located in the Canadian Arctic between Bathurst and Prince of Wales islands or about 807 miles (1,300 kilometers) from the geographic North Pole. The magnetic south pole moves around too. It was most recently recorded off the coast of Wilkes Land, Antarctica, roughly 1,584 miles (2,550 kilometers) from the geographical South Pole.

The lines of force that make up the Earth's magnetic field do not have a standard shape or regular pathway along the surface of the Earth; nor do they converge directly on the magnetic poles. Instead, they curve outward from the Earth and are blown around by the solar wind, a rain of electrically charged particles given off by the sun. The magnetic field also lacks a uniform strength. It is stronger near but not at the magnetic poles. Someone using a compass to find a magnetic pole will eventually reach the pole, but along the way will find that the needle, in response to a magnetic field of variable intensity, will send them along a roundabout path. If someone wanted to reach a destination between their starting point and a magnetic pole, they could easily miss it. To get a precise reading from a compass and to arrive at the intended destination, adjustments for these variations and disturbances must be made. Even when the Earth offers up assistance in establishing course and direction, the messages sent from the magnetic field must be interpreted in light of the many variables that could pull an expedition dangerously off course.

The Compass

Before the compass was introduced to the world of navigation, sailors had to depend almost completely on observation and the ever-changing

EARTH'S MAGNETIC FIELD IS GENERATED BY THE MOVEMENT OF MOLTEN IRON IN THE PLANET'S LIQUID OUTER CORE, DEPICTED IN YELLOW. THE MAGNETIC FIELD, REPRESENTED BY GRAY LINES, EXTENDS FROM AND CONVERGES AT THE MAGNETIC POLES, WHICH ARE LOCATED NEAR— BUT NOT PRECISELY AT—EARTH'S GEOGRAPHIC POLES.

moods of the winds. Sighting celestial bodies during the day and at night was a commonly used method. However, cloudy skies, among other atmospheric conditions, could easily make that method ineffective. A more reliable approach was needed.

Magnetite, a general name for magnetic substances, is a mineral that attracts iron and other metals. Magnetite ores are widely distributed in the Earth. Various peoples at different times in history discovered the ability of magnetite to attract other metals and align a metallic needle on a north–south axis. Navigators, inventors, and instrument makers learned to take advantage of the predictable pointing caused by these magnetic substances.

Chinese alchemists found that magnetite ore pointed south. Inventors figured out how to magnetize iron needles by rubbing them with magnetite. The Chinese also discovered that needles heated to a high temperature and then cooled when aligned with the north–south orientation of the Earth's axis would become magnetic.

It is not known for certain where the first compass appeared or whether it was invented in several places. In China, the first magnetic compass was made perhaps around the time of the Qin dynasty, which lasted from 221 to 206 BCE. This initial assemblage may have been just a bit of black magnetic rock placed on a piece of wood floating in a dish of water. Simple compasses took other forms as well. The magnetite was attached to a pointed shaft, for example, or allowed to hang from a silk thread.

The Chinese eventually produced a compass that lay on a flat surface bearing markings that indicated the directional points and the constellations. The magnetite pointer was shaped like a spoon. The rounded bowl-like end of the spoon rested on the flat surface, while the handle pointed south. Later, simple magnetized needles were used as well, starting in China in the eighth century CE.

By around 1100 CE the compass had come into common use among Chinese sailors as a valued navigational device. Zheng He (1371–1435), a Chinese navigator and diplomat of the Ming dynasty, is on record as

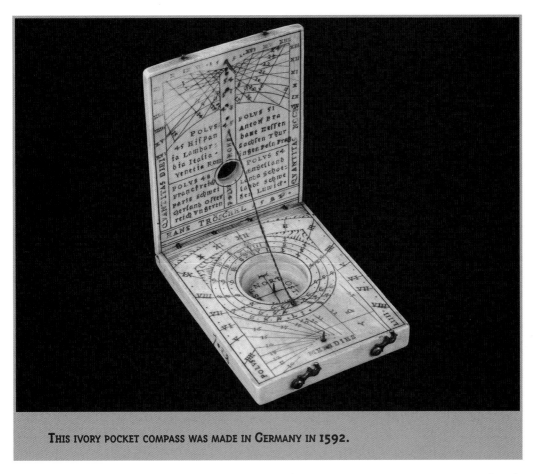

THIS IVORY POCKET COMPASS WAS MADE IN GERMANY IN 1592.

being the first person to have employed a compass as a navigational aid. Use of the compass soon spread, either through trade or war. Chinese and Mediterranean navigators in the eleventh and twelfth centuries relied on their compasses and the Earth's magnetism to chart and follow their courses. Arab mariners also turned to compasses for more accurate navigation and for guiding them during extended voyages across vast stretches of water.

In the 1300s, compasses were made with glass covers and an illustrated card under the needle that displayed thirty-two points of direction. This illustration, derived from the wind rose, came to be known as a compass rose. The individual points, each marking groups of the 360 degrees of a circle, reminded people of the many petals of a rose.

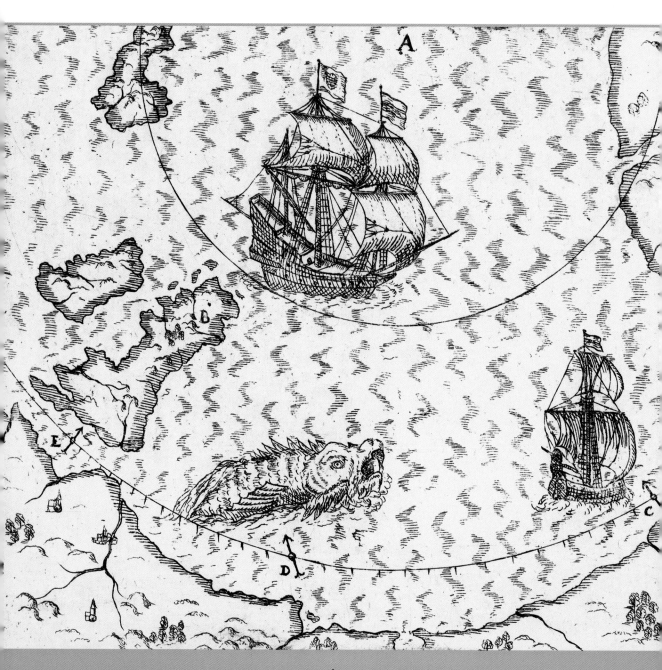

This engraving is from William Gilbert's *De magnete*, considered to be the first great scientific work published in England. The illustration presents a stylized vision of the North Sea, complete with sea monster, and accompanies the discussion of magnetic variations at sea.

Apprentice seamen were required to memorize the thirty-two compass points as part of their basic navigational knowledge. Naming them all, in order and without mistakes, to their superiors was known as boxing the compass. Today's navigators are trained to work with a 360-degree circle instead of directional names.

Although early adventurers did not understand the source of magnetism or the scientific principles underlying the compass, they knew they could rely on the fact that the needle or magnetized indicator would always point north and south. But compasses proved mystifying when they lost their magnetization for no apparent reason. Some superstitious seamen thought that eating strong-smelling foods such as garlic and onions could affect a compass. Since a ship's crew depended so heavily on their compass's accuracy, especially when they were far from their home shores, there were strict rules about who could use or get close to the compass.

The compass needle could also be misleading when a ship sailed into far northern or southern seas. Not until the mid-sixteenth century did seamen begin to recognize that the magnetic poles and the geographic poles were not in the same location. In the polar regions, this difference became magnified. There, though sailors might navigate according to their compass readings, they would find themselves to be far off course. A breakthrough in understanding magnetism and the behavior of the compass came in 1600 with the publication of *De magnete,* by William Gilbert. He conceived of the Earth as a giant magnet, having a magnetic field and magnetic poles distinct from the geographic poles. His insights helped to explain the movements of the compass needle: being magnetized, it aligned itself with Earth's magnetic poles—not its geographic poles.

Compass Corrections

In the 1600s, the narrow compass needle was abandoned for a wider pointer that could be more easily seen. Later, in 1745, English inventor Gowin Knight developed a compass with a steel needle that retained its magnetization for longer periods. Up to that time, the bits of magnetite used in compasses could become demagnetized if they were stored near large pieces of metal for too long. Other inventors suspended the needle in an air-filled brass container so that it swung freely. This type of compass became known as an air or standard compass.

Unfortunately, this design had problems that any child with a toy compass has observed. The air compass needle jiggles wildly and does not come to a stop quickly. The plans for modern navigational compasses solved this problem by designing a compass that was filled with a liquid that stops the needle from shaking and allows it to quickly point north. Today's compass manufacturers keep the formulas for these special liquids as company secrets.

Modern hand-held compasses also have a baseplate with lines for measuring distances on maps, a turning wheel for determining the location of distant objects, and a sighting mirror that allows the user to see the needle and a sighted object simultaneously. A contemporary mariner's compass can also have more than one magnetic needle attached to the card. Both move freely on a pivot point at the center of the compass. A mark on the card on the curved surface of the compass's base shows the ship's heading (the direction in which a ship is traveling).

A kind of compass error, known as deviation, is often caused by iron and steel materials located nearby. The iron fittings on a ship, for example, attract the magnetic needle of the compass and cause it to swing away from magnetic north. This deviation has to be corrected in order to get an accurate heading. To do so, a ship is aimed at a fixed point while its heading is recorded and aligned with fixed shore points. From these observations, a deviation key can be made that helps a navigator figure out the difference between what is magnetic north and where the compass is actually pointing and thus reduce error. Today's large ships do not depend completely on magnetic compass readings, but calculate heading and course with the help of more complex instruments.

GOWIN KNIGHT WROTE EXTENSIVELY ON MAGNETISM AND IMPROVED THE COMPASS, A DEVELOPMENT THE ROYAL NAVY EAGERLY WELCOMED.

Compasses Today

There are four main types of compasses used today. They are the simple compass, the mariner's compass, the digital compass, and the gyrocompass.

A simple compass is the version that many people carry when hiking. It can easily be slipped into a pocket or clipped onto a belt loop. This style has the traditional magnetic compass needle and a card with directional and 360 degree markings. These features make it possible to find your direction whether you are walking up a steep mountain, across a rocky beach, or staggering over scalding desert sands.

A mariner's compass is the type used on a ship. It is often covered with a clear glass compass bowl that is filled with a clear liquid. The liquid lets the card float and offers the compass stability so that the ship's movements do not alter or skew the reading with every roll. The needle of the mariner's compass pivots on a pin fixed below the card so that it can spin freely and always point to magnetic north.

The digital compass is becoming more common as standard equipment in motor vehicles. This type of compass works electronically to immediately alert drivers to changes in direction. Digital compasses, like other compasses, are affected by the Earth's magnetic field and by local magnetic conditions. To compensate, their electronic components make automatic adjustments when passing over a metal bridge, for example.

A gyrocompass is based on another important navigational device: the gyroscope. The compass is basically a kind of gyroscope, a device featuring a mounted, freely spinning wheel that can position itself in any manner. One major advantage of the gyrocompass is that it is able to determine the placement of geographic north, not magnetic north like other metal-based direction-finding aids.

The Gyroscope

The gyroscope was invented in the early 1800s. In 1852 the French scientist and physicist Jean Bernard Leon Foucault (1819–1868) gave the

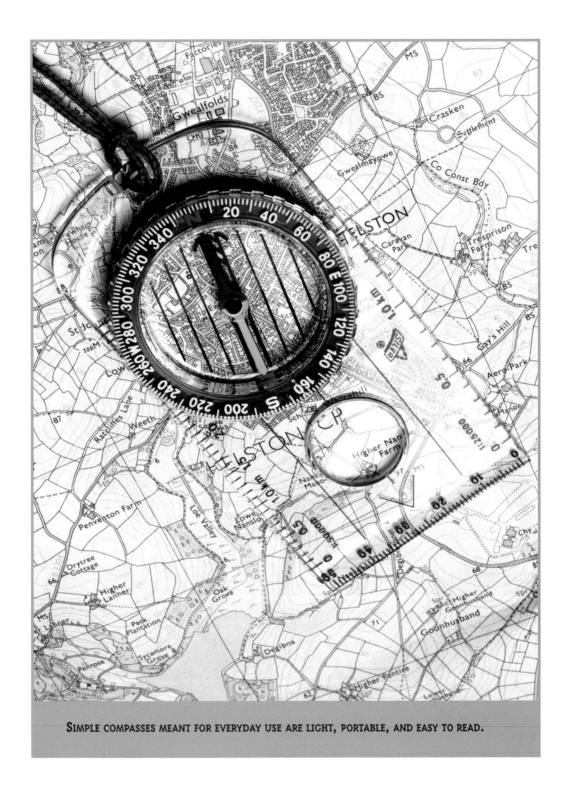

SIMPLE COMPASSES MEANT FOR EVERYDAY USE ARE LIGHT, PORTABLE, AND EASY TO READ.

IN ADDITION TO INVENTING THE GYROSCOPE, FRENCH PHYSICIST JEAN BERNARD LEON FOUCAULT ALSO DETERMINED THE VELOCITY OF LIGHT.

instrument its name. Initially Foucault used the gyroscope as a tool to study the Earth's rotation. Foucault's gyroscope was a revolving wheel mounted inside a set of rings. The rings could turn freely in any direction yet the wheel inside would maintain its upright position. This arrangement of freely moving supports is known as a gimbal.

A gyroscope's motion is related to Newton's first law of motion. This law states that an object in motion will continue to be in motion at a constant speed and in a straight line unless it is acted upon by another force.

The gyroscope became important to navigation because of its ability to keep its axis fixed even if it is bumped or subjected to other forces. To function as a gyrocompass, the axis of the gyroscope's spin is set to point at true geographic north. Unlike a magnetic compass, the gyrocompass's reading is not altered by the metals in the ship or by magnetic fields. Modern gyroscopes are driven by electric motors that keep them spinning at a steady speed.

The first gyrocompass was made in 1908 by Hermann Anschutz, a German who was working in England. Soon thereafter Elmer Sperry, an American inventor and industrialist, also developed a gyroscopic compass. Both men continued to perfect the device and to create variations with specific applications. During World War I, their gyrocompasses were installed in the ships of the United States and the Royal navies.

When two gyroscopes are mounted on a stand that is bolted inside a set of gimbals, with their axes at right angles to each other, the stand is able to remain stable even while the gimbals rotate in all directions. This is how an inertial navigation system works.

Within inertial navigation systems, sensors on the gimbals' axles identify when the stand rotates. The system then uses these signals from the sensor to record the vehicle's rotation in relation to its stand. When several speed-detecting sensors called accelerometers are also used, the inertial navigation system can detect a ship or airplane's heading as well as changes in direction.

Gyrocompasses are used to maintain course. The Sperry gyroscope

THE GYROSCOPE IS BUILT AROUND A CORE COMPONENT—A WHEEL SPINNING ON AN AXLE. IT IS A DEVICE USED FOR MAINTAINING A SHIP'S ORIENTATION.

acts as an automatic pilot and is today used in ships, airplanes, satellites, and spacecraft. It uses a gyroscope and sensors that are able to maintain a set course.

When starting a trip, the gyrocompass is set to north using a magnetic compass. The gyroscope has a motor that constantly corrects its chosen setting. Through gimbals and electronics, a gyroscope is able to keep a set course even when jostled or tilted by wind and the waves during a storm or rough seas.

The compass and the gyrocompass have brought the Earth's gravity and its self-generating and protective magnetic field into navigational service. These guides not only signal the direction in which a ship is traveling but also help to keep it on course.

PORTUGAL'S PRINCE HENRY WAS THE AUTHOR OF HIS NATION'S PLAN TO CONTROL AND
DOMINATE THE MARKETS OF THE EAST. HIS SCHOOL OF NAVIGATION PRODUCED SEAMEN WHO
WERE AMONG THE MOST EXPERIENCED AND CONFIDENT NAVIGATORS OF THE TIME.

Early Exploration

In the fifteenth century, Portugal was a major sea power. Portuguese ships manned by knowledgeable and brave sailors traveled regularly along the African coast to the Cape Verde Islands and the Indies. The person who encouraged Portugal's growing supremacy at sea was a powerful ruler, King João, known in English as King John.

In 1394 King João was blessed with the birth of his third son, the Infante Dom Henrique or Prince Henry. João spent time discussing his political and navigational dreams and strategies with Henry and his two brothers. Such talks first opened the young princes' eyes to the worlds that existed beyond their country's borders.

At nineteen, Prince Henry was sent north to build a fleet of ships in Oporto, Portugal, and to recruit, outfit, and train a force of sailors for his father's crusade to Ceuta in what is today called Morocco. While fulfilling his father's wishes, Henry acquired valuable experience and insight in the process. He learned navigational skills and heard much about the gold, spices, rugs, silver, and other trade items obtainable from the East.

Prince Henry, a devoutly religious soldier, became an important figure in the history of navigation. With the purpose of furthering the Christian faith, Henry's financing and patronage made many geographical discoveries possible. His interest in navigation encouraged trade and cultural contact among Europe, Africa, and the Far East. It is because of this increased expansion, that this era of Portuguese history is known as the time of the discoveries.

During this period of initial exploration, Portugal became an important center for nautical information. Merchants sought the advice of Portuguese navigators and captains before embarking on trading expeditions to far-off lands. During this busy time, the navigation school Henry started flourished and became known as an important center for studying all nautical matters. The brightest people in Europe came to Portuguese ports to study and to learn from the information brought back by various ships' captains and travelers from little-known regions. Dedicated students of the sea pieced together stories and observations to improve maps, sailing methods, and knowledge of the landmarks bordering distant waters. Learned men taught inexperienced sailors about the Atlantic currents and wind patterns and the newest navigational instruments and techniques.

As international navigation centers, Portuguese ports provided places for seafarers to compare experiences and work on common navigation problems. The populations of these towns included Muslims, Arabs, Germans, Scandinavians, and Italians from the seaports of Genoa and Venice.

To improve navigational techniques, however, experienced seamen had to take a look at the different factors that affected ocean travel. Not only did wandering off course get mariners lost, it caused collisions with ships that emerged unexpectedly from fog. Before ship-to-ship and ship-to-shore radio, accidents occurred from time to time, especially in narrow straits.

Despite the risks, undaunted seamen became more daring, and navigational knowledge benefited as a result. Whatever the source of their newfound courage, several captains had the confidence to pit themselves against unknown waters. For example, the farthest south that Europeans had traveled in the Atlantic Ocean in the early fifteenth century was Cape Bojador at latitude 27 degrees north (of the equator) in West Africa. Because of treacherous currents, no one had tried to go

VASCO DA GAMA GREW UP IN A TOWN ON THE COAST OF PORTUGAL, AMONG SAILORS AND FISHERMEN. THE SEA WAS A SECOND HOME TO HIM. HE HELD IT AMONG HIS GREATEST ACHIEVEMENTS THAT HE WAS ABLE TO FULFILL PRINCE HENRY'S DREAM OF FINDING A SEA ROUTE TO THE EAST.

beyond that boundary. Most of the crews that had tried to take longer voyages had never made it back to tell their stories. One Portuguese adventurer who put his navigational skills to the test was Gil Eanes of Lagos. He became the first European sea captain to round Cape Bojador and then return in 1434.

Prince Henry's death in 1460 did not prevent further Portuguese successes. Bartolomeu Dias rounded the Cape of Good Hope in 1488. Vasco da Gama, another brave Portuguese explorer, completed a sea route to India in 1498.

Christopher Columbus is reported to have been shipwrecked off the coast of Portugal in 1476, when the twenty-four-year-old's ship

Dead Reckoning

To find a ship's position, the captain measured the speed and the direction in which it had traveled from its previous position. This was called deduced reckoning or "ded" reckoning. Later it became known as "dead" reckoning. The method was developed to estimate a ship's new position. Dead reckoning came into use on long voyages after the compass became a standard navigational aid.

Like other sailors of the time, Columbus's crew measured the ship's speed by throwing a piece of flotsam (usually a thin piece of wood) over the side of the ship. By using two marks on the ship's rail, placed at a specific distance from each other, sailors could measure the time it took the flotsam to float from the front of the ship to the back. From this time, the ship's speed could then be calculated. This method of measuring speed was used by Dutch mariners and became known as the Dutchman's log.

A reading of the speed and direction of the ship was taken hourly and recorded in a journal called a log. At the end of each day, the ship's total distance and course were noted on the chart and compared with the intended course. Dead reckoning gave sailors an idea of whether they were on course or needed to make corrections. It helped them to note if the winds or the currents had moved them off course. However, dead reckoning had its limitations. Since dead reckoning depended on finding the distance traveled (calculating the time and speed) and on setting a daily course, the measurements of speed and direction had to be accurate. Obtaining the flotsam's speed did not work well when there was little or no wind and the ship was moving slowly, if at all. Compass readings could vary, as could timekeeping.

The log of Columbus's first transatlantic voyage in 1492 still exists. From his notes, naval historians know that Columbus navigated by dead reckoning. His landfall in the New World was unexpected, but by using dead reckoning he was able to recross the Atlantic, go back to Spain, and then make return voyages to approximately the same locations in the Americas.

was attacked by pirates. Columbus swam 6 miles (9.7 kilometers) to the Portuguese shore. From there he later set off for Lisbon. His ensuing passion for exploring new lands has been linked in part to the time he spent in the Portuguese ports and in Lisbon.

It is suspected that because of Prince Henry's influence, Portuguese astronomers in 1480 figured out how to determine latitude by using the sun's position as it moves north and south of the equator with the seasons. This phenomenon is called declination.

A statue of Prince Henry the Navigator faces the harbor at Lagos, Portugal, in a square where Henry's palace once stood before it was destroyed in an earthquake in 1755. Many portions of the old city walls are also intact, along with a statue of Gil Eanes, the explorer who left Lagos to round Cape Bojador, the end of the known world at that time.

Around the World

After initial and increasing Portuguese successes, many ships subsequently set sail each year from the port of Belixe on the Atlantic coast of Portugal. Each expedition went a little farther than its predecessors did along the huge navigational challenge that lay off the west coast of Africa. These voyagers laid the foundations for Portugal's increasing international influence.

Ferdinand Magellan (1480–1521) was a Portuguese sea captain who had fallen out of favor with his king. He went to a rival, Charles I of Spain, in search of funding for his expedition to find a new route to the Spice Islands, which lay north of Australia. In 1519 Charles I gave him five ships and 265 men to undertake the mission.

It took Magellan three months, from September 8 to December 13, 1519, to sail down the coast of Africa and cross the Atlantic Ocean to South America. He then sailed slowly south, exploring the bays and rivers to see if one of them offered a way through the continent. After stopping for the winter, the fleet, at the time made up of four ships— one having been lost—resumed its southerly course. The ships entered what was later named the Strait of Magellan on October 21, 1520, to

SAILING FOR SPAIN, FERDINAND MAGELLAN'S EXPEDITION WAS THE FIRST TO SAIL AROUND THE GLOBE. IT TOOK THE FEW SURVIVING CREW MEMBERS ALMOST THREE YEARS TO MAKE THE VOYAGE.

cross the tip of South America. After a month, three ships, one ship having turned back for Spain, emerged into the Pacific Ocean. Magellan then sailed north across the Pacific, but naturally he had no sense of the great size of the ocean, a body of water bigger than all the combined land surface on Earth. Magellan thought Asia would be a few hundred miles past the coast of South America, but the voyage stretched approximately 12,600 miles (20,286 kilometers) before reaching first the Mariana Islands and then the Philippines on the other side of the Pacific.

Although Magellan is given credit for leading the first expedition to circumnavigate or circle the globe, he did not live to complete the journey. It was just bad luck that after surviving severe storms, fighting between the Portuguese and Spanish crew members of the expedition, mutinies, and near starvation when food stores dipped dangerously low, a skirmish in the Philippines claimed his life. Although welcomed by the native peoples, Magellan became entangled in local affairs. Siding with one local king, Magellan led a charge with sixty men against a rival ruler who turned out to have more than a thousand men. Magellan was killed during the battle on Mactan Island in 1521.

Despite the fact that Magellan did not return to Spain, he had discovered a passage between the Atlantic and the Pacific oceans at the tip of South America. Passing through the strait, he and his crew were the first Europeans to sail into the Pacific Ocean. Magellan named the vast body of water Pacific (which means "peaceful") because its waters seemed calm after the stormy Atlantic. It is ironic that the Strait of Magellan and the Pacific Ocean are known since for their fierce winds, huge waves, and intense weather.

After Magellan's death, it took the crew, under the command of Juan Sebastian Elcano, until 1522 to finish the voyage around the globe. Of the 265 original members, eighteen men made it back to their home port in Spain with a rich cargo of spices, including expensive cloves. The men were filled with stories of the wondrous sights they had seen. Magellan's crew reported new species of camels without humps (either llamas or alpacas) and a goose that could not be plucked before cooking, but must

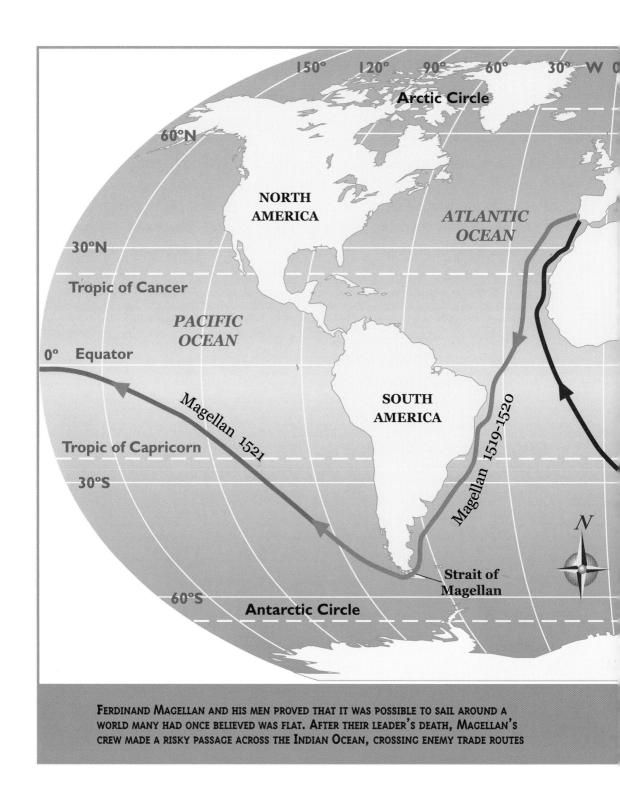

150° 120° 90° 60° 30° W 0°

Arctic Circle

60°N

NORTH
AMERICA

ATLANTIC
OCEAN

30°N

Tropic of Cancer

PACIFIC
OCEAN

0° Equator

Magellan 1521

SOUTH
AMERICA

Magellan 1519-1520

Tropic of Capricorn

30°S

N

Strait of
Magellan

60°S

Antarctic Circle

FERDINAND MAGELLAN AND HIS MEN PROVED THAT IT WAS POSSIBLE TO SAIL AROUND A
WORLD MANY HAD ONCE BELIEVED WAS FLAT. AFTER THEIR LEADER'S DEATH, MAGELLAN'S
CREW MADE A RISKY PASSAGE ACROSS THE INDIAN OCEAN, CROSSING ENEMY TRADE ROUTES

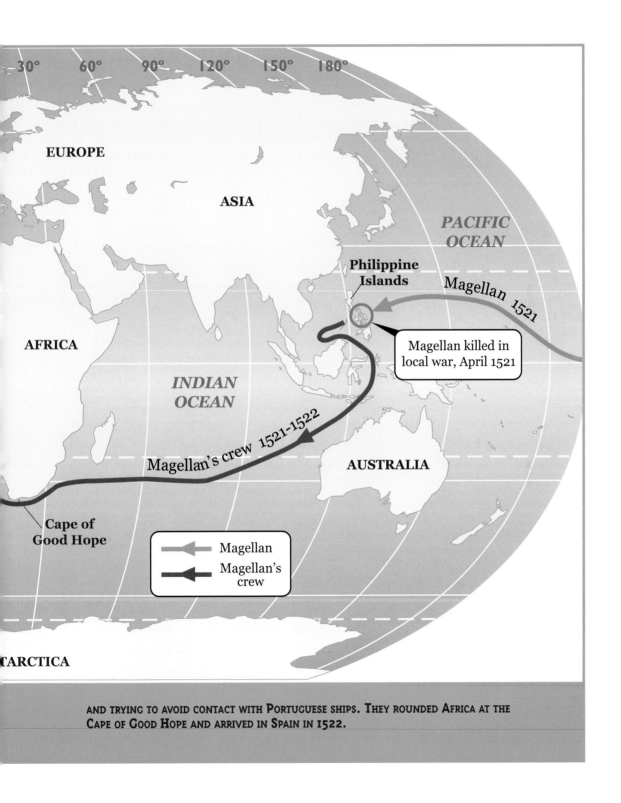

30° 60° 90° 120° 150° 180°

EUROPE

ASIA

PACIFIC
OCEAN

Philippine
Islands

Magellan 1521

Magellan killed in
local war, April 1521

AFRICA

INDIAN
OCEAN

Magellan's crew 1521-1522

AUSTRALIA

Cape of
Good Hope

Magellan
Magellan's
crew

ARCTICA

AND TRYING TO AVOID CONTACT WITH PORTUGUESE SHIPS. THEY ROUNDED AFRICA AT THE
CAPE OF GOOD HOPE AND ARRIVED IN SPAIN IN 1522.

DEE CAFFARI IS THE FIRST WOMAN TO SAIL AROUND THE WORLD AGAINST THE PREVAILING WINDS AND CURRENTS. HERE HER HISTORIC JOURNEY ENDS IN SOUTHAMPTON, ENGLAND, IN MAY 2006.

be skinned (a penguin). Moreover, two of the closest galaxies, the Magellanic Clouds, were discovered by crew members while in the Southern Hemisphere.

Magellan's ambitious voyage, guided by an astrolabe, an hourglass, and a compass, offered solid proof that the Earth was round and much larger than expected. It also demonstrated the usefulness of celestial navigational aids and opened the door to those wary seamen who needed to be certain of their route before starting a long journey.

Modern Adventures

Since Magellan's journey, the globe has been circumnavigated many times. Some of these voyages were performed with a full crew, while others were done single-handedly. Although early expeditions had only the most basic navigational aids available, modern excursions have usually been aided by satellite imagery, telephone, radar, and precise maps. Wandering around without hope or food is no longer as common as it was in centuries past.

A recent successful attempt to circumnavigate the globe alone was completed in 2006 by Dee Caffari. The voyage took 178 days and was not always an easy one. Her grueling 29,297-mile (47,168-kilometer) adventure around the globe was accomplished despite violent storms, icebergs, doldrums (no wind), and occasional visits by migrating or lost birds. Thirty-two-year-old Caffari, an experienced English yachtswoman and former secondary-school physical education teacher, said the daily e-mails she received kept her going when the sailing was especially difficult or slow. For some people, the realities and pitfalls of ocean travel are universal and timeless.

GREEK ASTRONOMER AND MATHEMATICIAN PTOLEMY, AS PORTRAYED BY FIFTEENTH-CENTURY ARTIST JOOS VAN GHENT. NAVIGATIONAL CHARTS HAVE BEEN ESSENTIAL TO SAILORS EVER SINCE PTOLEMY CREATED THE FIRST WORLD MAPS IN THE SECOND CENTURY CE, COMPLETE WITH LATITUDE AND LONGITUDE LINES.

Maps and Charts

Although people first knew that the Earth was round about 2,500 years ago, that realization was somehow forgotten along the way. The Greeks were the first to determine the correct shape of the Earth. Scholars such as Pythagoras in 500 BCE noticed that the altitudes of stars were higher or lower at different places on the Earth's surface and that ships appeared little by little over the horizon as they got closer to shore. As a ship returned to port, first the top of its mast, then the sails, and finally its hull came slowly into view. It would not happen that way and in that order if the Earth were flat.

Aristotle, who lived about 300 BCE reported that the Earth cast a rounded shadow on the moon. Other early Greeks calculated the Earth's size and developed a grid system of latitude and longitude that provided two coordinates with which to find any point on the Earth. Greek sailors began to use charts based on this grid system to plan their voyages.

Around 150 CE Claudius Ptolemy, a Greek mathematician and astronomer, consulted the archives at the library in Alexandria, Egypt, and wrote an encyclopedia detailing the knowledge of the ancient world. This eight-volume work included instructions for drawing maps of the world that were based on the notion of a curved globe located at the center of the universe.

Unfortunately, between 400 and 1200 Greek knowledge was neglected and lost as the Western world entered the Dark Ages. Learning was viewed with suspicion. Maps made at the time were based on rumor and guesswork, not on observations, calculations, or scientific understanding. Illustrated maps with the "four corners of the Earth" warned seamen of the dangers of venturing too far from home.

Luckily, the Arab world retained Ptolemy's groundbreaking work. His writings were rediscovered by Western scholars when Europe entered the Middle Ages. His work was translated into Latin. Ptolemy's explanations of how to draw a sphere on a flat piece of paper made it possible for map makers and explorers to record newly discovered lands and ocean routes. The invention of the printing press in 1440 also

A SEA SERPENT MAKES A MEAL OF AN UNLUCKY NORWEGIAN SAILOR. SUCH FANCIFUL AND OFTEN FRIGHTENING DEPICTIONS HELPED EXPRESS A FEAR OF THE UNKNOWN MANY EARLY NAVIGATORS WERE FORCED TO OVERCOME—OR IGNORE—ON THEIR OFTEN LIFE-THREATENING VOYAGES.

allowed more people to use and update maps as new information became more widely known.

To add to their charts and maps, mariners kept notebooks in which they recorded the features of the sea routes. Called a *portolano,* the guidebook listed such things as the distances between coastal landmarks and the best approaches to ports.

As more mariners came to use the compass in the 1300s, rhumb lines were added to the sailors' charts and maps to show the direction to take from one port to the other. This type of chart, called a portulan chart, often included a compass rose to establish the directions and the orientation of the chart. Along the way, navigators used the *portolano* and the portulan chart to track their ship's progress. Lines were sketched between points on the chart to show the ship's course as indicated by dead reckoning and as a way of checking against the course prescribed by the chart maker. From the scale of measurement on the chart, the distance traveled could be calculated.

Map makers also often included drawings of sea monsters on their maps. The cartographers based their drawings on descriptions of sea creatures from as early as the 1300s, when long-distance sailing first became possible. Sea monster sightings were shown on the map in roughly the same area where they had been claimed to have been originally spotted. Illustrations of whalelike monsters and hideous marine creatures marked places to avoid.

Maps and charts have been valued since the earliest days of navigation. They were seen as assurances of safety by seamen who relied on the experiences and accuracy of others. A detailed navigational chart or map, drawn to scale, of a specific geographical area was a great aid to sailors crossing vast stretches of water. Cartography became an esteemed career, and map makers often formed important craft guilds in harbor cities.

While essential, maps, the most basic of navigational aids and often taken for granted today, were not easily obtained centuries ago. Monarchs of seafaring countries demanded that accurate descriptions of

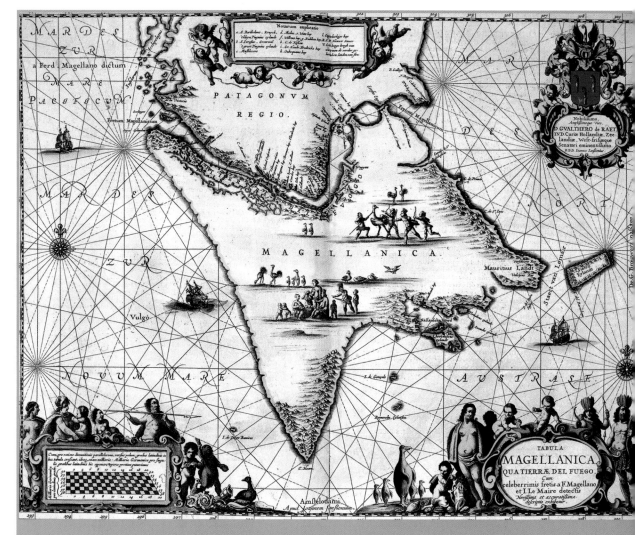

THIS MAP FROM THE 1650S SHOWS THE SOUTHERN TIP OF SOUTH AMERICA, INCLUDING THE STRAIT OF MAGELLAN. MAPS WERE PRIZED FOR THEIR PRACTICALITY AND THE INFORMATION THEY CONTAINED. THE DECORATIVE AND ARTISTIC ELEMENTS PRESENT ON MANY EARLY MAPS INDICATE HOW HIGHLY VALUED SUCH DOCUMENTS WERE.

newly discovered lands and inland waterways be provided to the map makers after a ship returned to port. Kings and queens were eager to fill their treasuries with wealth derived from the new trade routes. So it was critical that the specific landmarks such as reefs, cliffs, and rocky shorelines be recorded to provide a guide to later seamen sailing on the royal payroll. Subsequent expeditions could not reach the same destination as the exploratory ships if navigators did not know whether to avoid a group of islands or sail through them. The accuracy of charts and the information they provided meant the success or failure of trading ventures to far-flung regions.

Not only did navigational maps improve the chances of a safe passage, they were greatly valued in themselves. Often maps were sold with land grants to wealthy adventurers who wanted to own a piece of the newly discovered territories they explored. With a purchased map in hand, aristocratic explorers would set off to establish settlements and colonies, regardless of the native people who already lived on the newly acquired land.

Today maps continue to play an often indispensable role in our daily navigational needs. Turn right? Continue straight ahead? Without the accurate guidance maps provide, an outing or visit to a new place could quickly turn into chaos and confusion. Although some maps have transcended their traditional paper bounds to appear in electronic form on computer screens and hand-held devices, maps remain essential tools, representations of where we've been and where we're going.

LINES OF LATITUDE AND LONGITUDE CRISSCROSS AND SUBDIVIDE EARTH'S SURFACE.

The Imaginary Grid

The globe has long been portrayed with lines of longitude running north and south and with perpendicular lines of latitude running east and west. This imaginary grid divides the surface of the Earth into quadrants and allows navigators a reliable means of establishing position and direction. Latitude lines run parallel to the equator; for this reason, they are also called parallels of latitude. If you start at the North Pole, draw ever-larger concentric rings encircling the planet, you eventually get to the equator. The same thing happens in reverse from the equator to the South Pole. The circles become smaller the farther from the equator they are, eventually ending in the points marked by the geographic poles.

When finding latitude, measurements are made from the equator either northward or southward. The equator is at 0 degrees latitude. The latitude of the North Pole is 90 degrees N, and the South Pole is 90 degrees S. Every point of latitude in between is measured as a particular degree north or south, from 0 degrees to 90 degrees. One degree of latitude equals about 69 miles (111 kilometers).

Geographers realized that in order to pinpoint a specific location, a system of coordinates was needed that established where two lines met—one running east-west and another running north-south. In this way, the concept of longitude was born.

Longitudinal lines, which run north and south and meet at the poles, are known as meridians. The meridian that runs through Greenwich, England, is known as the line of 0 degrees longitude or the prime meridian. It serves as the starting point for counting degrees of longitude to the east and to the west. This means that one half of the globe is measured in degrees of east longitude up to 180, and the other half is measured in degrees of west longitude up to 180. Longitude is sometimes labeled with the Greek letter $\bar{I}$ or *Lo* on maps, but more commonly, the words *east* or *west* are used.

Knowing a ship's exact latitude and longitude allows a sailor to identify its precise location on the

THE PRIME MERIDIAN, 0 DEGREES LONGITUDE, RUNS THROUGH GREENWICH, ENGLAND, AMONG MANY OTHER PLACES.

Earth's waterways, oceans, and seas. Both latitude and longitude are measured in terms of the 360 degrees that make up a circle. One degree is equal to 60 minutes, which can then be further subdivided.

The system of latitude and longitude has proved invaluable to the success of many kinds of excursions, from military operations to trade voyages to recreational outings. However, it took navigators many years to arrive at an easy way to determine their longitude wherever they happened to find themselves in the world.

The main problem facing early mariners on the open seas was the difficulty of determining both latitude and longitude, especially when they were in unfamiliar waters and on long-distance voyages. While it was easier for experienced sailors to gauge distance and direction when they traveled north and south of the equator, it was difficult for them to determine how far they had traveled east or west. They could find their latitude by checking the altitude of the sun or some other heavenly body, but they did not have a dependable way of reading longitude. Over a long distance, the curvature of the Earth affected their measurements to a greater extent and was not always properly taken note of in the complicated calculations needed to determine longitude. Accurate timekeeping was also needed to determine longitude, which was not possible until the eighteenth century.

Keeping Time at Sea

The ordered grid that subdivides the world into mapable parcels is taken for granted today. Finding a way to figure out longitude proved to be a significant challenge to eighteenth-century scientists and navigators. Sea captains, explorers, and merchants petitioned England's Parliament in 1714 to come up with a means of accurately determining longitude. In response to this growing concern over the lack of precision, Parliament offered a cash prize to anyone who could find a reliable way of calculating longitude at sea. A Board of Longitude was established to oversee the challenge.

The awards being offered were appealing—10,000 pounds, the British unit of currency, if within one degree of the correct position, 15,000 if accurate to within two-thirds of a degree, and up to 20,000 if within one-half of a degree. This was a significant amount of money in the 1700s, so several ingenious people set about trying to solve the longitude problem.

What was required was coming up with a means of telling time simultaneously at sea and at a fixed location (such as Greenwich, England) as well. Sailors could usually measure local time by observing the sun. Pendulum clocks, which had achieved a high degree of reliability by the seventeenth century, could be brought onboard, but the tilting of the ship and changes in temperature and humidity prevented the clocks from keeping accurate time once at sea. No matter how the time was determined, accurate navigation required that seafarers know the time at a standard position in order to calculate their longitude. The differences

A SAILOR'S INABILITY TO ACCURATELY DETERMINE LONGITUDE WHILE AT SEA WAS LINKED TO AN ESSENTIAL PROBLEM OF TIMEKEEPING. TO FIGURE OUT A SHIP'S LONGITUDE, MARINERS HAD TO KNOW THE EXACT TIME NOT ONLY ONBOARD BUT AT A FIXED LOCATION ELSEWHERE. THE SIMPLE CLOCKS OF THE DAY WERE THROWN OFF BY THE MOTION OF THE OCEAN'S CURRENTS AND WAVES, A PROBLEM THAT WOULD BE UNTHINKABLE IN TODAY'S MODERN VERSIONS.

between the two local times could then be used to determine how far apart—east or west—the locations were.

Another method of determining longitude proved to be beyond the mathematical abilities of most practitioners of the time. King Charles II founded the Royal Observatory at Greenwich in 1675 with the original intent of establishing an accurate listing of the positions of the stars. If sailors figured out the position of the moon relative to the known location of a particular star, the moon's motion could then be used to calculate what is referred to as Greenwich Mean Time. This method turned out to be challenging, however, because it required accurate tables of the moon's various positions as it crosses the sky. More reliable lunar tables, published by John Napier in 1614 and by Tobias Mayer in 1755, helped this method, but the calculations and more complex measurements required proved too difficult for most mariners. Inexact knowledge of the stars' positions as well as poor instruments for measuring the distances between the stars and the moon only added to problem. The challenge of determining longitude would not be solved until the late eighteenth century.

John Hadley and Thomas Godfrey aided the attempt to find a way of accurately determining longitude by independently developing the sextant, an instrument that could more accurately determine the moon's position. But it was a Yorkshire carpenter and self-taught clock maker who would ultimately claim the Board of Longitude's prize. John Harrison had developed a series of clocks for telling time at sea. He created a large silver watch known as H.4 in 1759, which was tested by the

A SMALL AND MODEST WATCH LIES BESIDE INVENTOR JOHN HARRISON IN THIS EIGHTEENTH-CENTURY ENGRAVING. SOME ACQUAINTANCES REFERRED TO HIM AS LONGITUDE HARRISON, ACKNOWLEDGING HIS CONTRIBUTIONS TO THE HISTORY OF NAVIGATION.

Board of Longitude on a 1762 voyage to Jamaica and a 1764 journey to Barbados. Harrison's H.4 finally solved the problem that had stumped sailors for centuries. His chronometer, as the device was called, kept the time of a known fixed location, a measurement that could then serve as a reference point for determining the ship's position. The invaluable instrument marked another significant turning point in the history of navigation and helped to begin an era marked by even more daring voyages to still-unknown pockets of the world.

THIS LITHOGRAPH FROM THE 1880S PRESENTS AN ARTIST'S VISION OF THE LIGHTHOUSE AT ALEXANDRIA.

SEVEN

Lighting the Way

No matter how experienced or brave a navigator was, finding his position at night—with only the moon or stars as beacons—was challenging. Over time, watch fires and light towers were built along coastal areas—the earliest-known attempts at improving night navigation. The structures were set high above tough-to-navigate waters near reefs, cliffs, channels, and sandbars or served as warnings to vessels that ship-shattering rocks were close by. But the fires required a lot of wood and constant tending in order to be helpful. Bad weather also rendered them useless.

The earliest known lighthouse, built in ancient Egypt under Ptolemy Soter—who ruled about 280 BCE—was located in Alexandria. The huge stone expanse of the Pharos lighthouse was estimated to be about 400 feet (122 meters) high and was the third-tallest structure in the world at the time, after the Great Pyramid and Khafre's Pyramid, both at Giza.

The Pharos lighthouse's shining stonework reflected the sun during the day. At night, fires reportedly seen more than 30 miles (48 kilometers) away were lit to warn incoming and passing vessels. It is unclear whether the fires were built every night, only during moonless nights, or when specific ships were expected. Invaders may also have benefited from the Pharos's bright beacon.

For thousands of years, ancient lighthouses used fire to produce their lights. But building a signal blaze was useless or impossible in high winds or rain. Still, fire was the easiest way to create a warning beacon. Later on, some lighthouses burned coal, but most continued to use wood. Eventually candles shielded with glass lanterns were found to burn brighter, while having the added benefit of being protected from the elements. Overall, few improvements were introduced to the world's growing number of lighthouses until the late seventeenth century, when the glass-encased lantern room was invented and installed in England's Eddystone Lighthouse. That beacon sits on a pile of ship-wrecking rocks 14 miles (23 kilometers) out to sea, southwest of Plymouth.

Wooden bowls lined with mirrors were also introduced. They were placed upright behind oil lamps to serve as reflectors and as a means of directing the light. These innovations produced more light, but shipwrecks continued because captains could not see the warning light until the danger was upon them. Brighter, more reliable lights were needed.

In 1783 Swiss scientist Aimé Argand is believed to have first used reflectors to make the beam of light appear brighter. Around the same time, Argand also invented a long-burning oil lamp that eliminated the need for feeding the fires all night.

Although lighthouse reflector systems from the late 1700s to the early 1800s marked significant strides in replacing open fires and candles in lantern rooms, the inventions only captured, reflected, and effectively redirected a small percentage of the light. Additional improvement was required.

Augustin Fresnel, a French physicist experimenting with the behavior of light and the theory of wave optics, introduced perhaps the most significant innovation in navigational lighting. In 1819 he wrote a paper on the diffraction of light (the redirection of light waves) for which he received a prize from the Académie des Sciences in Paris. Fresnel later became a member of the academy, as well as a member of the Royal Society of London. He was also made the commissioner of lighthouses in France, which led to his work on building mirrors to use in lighthouses instead of fire.

A FRAIL SCIENTIST WITH AN INTEREST IN OPTICS, AUGUSTIN FRESNEL PREVENTED COUNTLESS WRECKS AND DEATHS WITH THE DEVELOPMENT OF HIS LENS—A SERIES OF TIERED PRISMS THAT COULD CREATE AND EMIT A POWERFUL BEAM.

Lighthouse Milestones

Importance	Location	Date
First American lighthouse	Boston, Massachusetts	1716
Oldest original lighthouse still in service	Sandy Hook, New Jersey	1764
Newest lighthouse	Charleston, South Carolina	1962
Only triangular-shaped lighthouse tower	Charleston, South Carolina	1962
Second most powerful lighthouse in the world	Charleston, South Carolina	1962
Tallest lighthouse (191 feet—58 meters)	Cape Hatteras, North Carolina	1870
Highest lighthouse (515 feet—157 meters—above sea level)	Cape Mendocino, California	1868
First American-built West coast lighthouse	Alcatraz Island, California	1854
First lighthouse to use electricity	Statue of Liberty, New York, NY	1886
First Great Lakes lighthouses	Buffalo, New York/Erie, PA	1818
Most expensive lighthouse (adjusted cost)	Saint George's Reef, California	1891
First lighthouse built completely by the U.S. government	Montauk Point, New York	1797

SOLDIERS POSE AT THE BASE OF THE
BADLY DAMAGED LIGHTHOUSE ON
MORRIS ISLAND, SOUTH CAROLINA,
AFTER THE 1863 SIEGE OF
CHARLESTON, ONE OF THE MILITARY
ACTIONS THAT MARKED THE U.S.
CIVIL WAR.

Since Fresnel focused his attention on the nature of light itself, his studies and their practical application led to the most important invention in lighthouse illumination in more than two thousand years. Through his calculations, Fresnel figured out how light changes direction, or refracts, when passing through a glass prism. After meeting with the most advanced glass makers of his time, he had a lens created that was formed by an arrangement of several prisms. The Fresnel lens used a large lamp as its light source and contained magnifying glasses surrounded above and below by concentric rings of prisms and mirrors. These were all perfectly angled to gather and increase the intensity of the light. Fresnel's complex series of lenses created a single concentrated beam of brilliant light that could be seen for miles.

Fresnel's lens was much more efficient at collecting and directing light than earlier lenses had been. It created a beam five times more powerful than that produced by the reflector systems used in lighthouses. To take advantage of the light's high intensity, the lens system was installed at the highest point possible, so the light could be seen from a great distance before it was hidden by the curvature of the Earth. When mounted at 100 feet (31 meters) above sea level, a Fresnel light could be seen up to 18 miles (29 kilometers) away.

Fresnel lenses are ranked by size or order. A first-order lens, with more than 1,000 prisms, was from 10 to 12 feet (3 to 3.7 meters) tall, measured 6 feet (1.8 meters) around, and weighed up to 3 tons (2.7 metric tons). These powerful lenses were used in lighthouses along foggy coasts or above dangerous rocky cliffs. The weakest lens, a sixth-order lens, was mostly used in lights on lakes and harbors.

The first Fresnel lens was mounted in the Cardovan Tower lighthouse on France's Gironde River in 1822. Its light could be seen more than 20 miles (32 kilometers) away.

In 1907 a Fresnel lens almost 6 feet (1.9 meters) tall and more than 3 feet (0.9 meter) wide was installed in the Bolivar Lighthouse near Galveston, Texas. This Fresnel lens contained several rows of prisms and looked like a crystal beehive. It was in service during the terrible

ONE OF THE UNITED STATES' MOST ICONIC LIGHTHOUSES—THE STRIPED BEACON FOUND ON
CAPE HATTERAS, NORTH CAROLINA.

Galveston hurricane of 1900 when many local inhabitants sought refuge in the lighthouse from a storm that would claim more than six thousand lives. The Bolivar light and its Fresnel lens are now located inside the Hall of American Maritime Enterprise at the National Museum of American History in Washington, D.C.

Lighthouses cropped up across the coastal United States. They were erected at important points and on hazardous stretches of coastline. They were manned by keepers who made sure that the nighttime light was never extinguished. This lonely job was often held by retired seamen who were familiar with local navigational hazards and who kept plenty of kerosene oil on hand for use in the lamps.

The first lighthouse in what would be the United States was finished in 1716, on Little Brewster Island in Boston Harbor. It is reported to have cost 12,000 dollars (a hefty sum at the time) and is still in operation, though with a newer tower and light. Now called Boston Light, its white tower is 89 feet (27 meters) tall and flashes a beam every 10 seconds that is visible for 27 miles (43 kilometers).

In the last century, the eastern coast of the United States was dotted with lighthouses of many types and color. They could be recognized during the day by their color, shape, or stripes. At night, sailors could identify the lighthouses by the color of their lights (white, red, or green), by the time it took to finish a full cycle or sequence of flashes, and by the number and duration of the light and dark intervals. Approximately ninety classic Fresnel-type lenses remain in use in lighthouses as active navigational aids today.

Lighthouses are classified as major or minor. A light is categorized according to its height and the maximum range or distance that the light can be cast. Major lighthouses include the tallest ones and those with the strongest lights, the ones most important to local navigation, and ones built in particularly treacherous waters along routes used by incoming and outgoing ships. Either way, big or small, lighthouses have served as essential beacons, guiding safe passage for hundreds of years.

Navigating Coastal Waters

All kinds of vessels compete for space along coasts and especially in major ports and harbors. To prevent collisions, sailors, pilots, navies, and even local and national governmental agencies have developed markers and codes that identify hazards, direct the course of sea traffic, and make ships easier to see. Some of these systems—such as buoys and beacons—float in the water, while others—such as lights on a ship—travel with the vessels on which they are installed.

Buoys

A buoy is a floating marker that indicates the location of shoals, or underwater rocks, or the boundaries of a channel through which ships may safely pass. Buoys are anchored to the seafloor to keep them in place, and each buoy is usually weighted on the bottom to keep it upright. Buoys have a variety of shapes, colors, and markings that convey additional information. They may also be equipped with bells, whistles, foghorns, or lights to make them more noticeable in bad weather and at night. Even when out of visible range, buoys and beacons equipped with radar signals may be detected by a ship.

Buoys have been used for centuries but they do not always show up in documents or histories. One of the earliest records, from the thirteenth century, notes the use of buoys in the Guadalquivir River, where they directed mariners to the port city of Seville, Spain.

CREW MEMBERS ROUND A BUOY DURING A RACE OFF THE COAST OF ENGLAND. NAVIGATIONAL MARKERS PROVIDE ORDER AND ENCOURAGE SAFE PASSAGE.

The first buoys were often wooden casks anchored to the seafloor with chains and large stones. There were also simple spar buoys, poles stuck into the seafloor or, in other forms, weighted at one end and attached to the bottom. Local port authorities were in charge of maintenance and collected fees from mariners and merchants for the buoys' repair and upkeep. As a consequence, the size, shape, color, and placement of buoys, and what these various codes signified, varied from place to place. As a result, those ports well marked with buoys often had orderly sea traffic, while other less equipped harbors were not as well organized.

One attempt to oversee navigational aids on a national level came in 1514, when England's King Henry VIII granted a charter for that purpose to the Guild of Shipmen and Mariners. The royal order led to the formation of Trinity House, the agency in the British government that manages all of the navigational aids placed in British waters. Not until 1594, however, did Queen Elizabeth I grant the guild the right to install buoys.

For the American colonies, as their economies and trade volume grew, it was important to ensure safe sea lanes and harbor approaches. Numerous lighthouses were built, and records show that cask buoys were used in the Delaware River, and spar buoys were installed in Boston Harbor. After the colonies won their independence from England, one of the first acts passed by the new Congress, in 1789, established federal support for the maintenance of lighthouses, buoys, beacons, and public piers. This responsibility was assigned to the Department of the Treasury. In 1938 the U.S. Coast Guard assumed the duty.

The United States did not at first have a standardized system when it came to the size and look of buoys. Their shape, color, and size varied from one port to the next. By the mid-1800s, captains were complaining that the existing buoys were too small to be seen at a distance, a concern that gained in importance as ships increased in size and, powered by steam, traveled at faster speeds. Eventually a more uniform

BUOYS ARE DESIGNED TO BE DURABLE AND TO REQUIRE LITTLE OR NO MAINTENANCE. THESE BEACHED BUOYS WERE GIVEN A RARE COAT OF FRESH PAINT, DECORATED BY AN ARTIST TO RESEMBLE THE CHINESE FLAG.

system came into use as America's coastal waters continued to bustle with trade and to fill with vessels from around the world.

This is the result of the U.S. Congress's 1848 adoption of what is called the lateral system or the "red, right, return" system. When a ship returns to a harbor, red buoys are on the starboard or right-hand side of a channel and black buoys are on the port or left-hand side. Since then, green was found to have greater visibility than black, and in the 1970s the black buoys were replaced with green ones.

In 1982 the United States and many other seagoing nations agreed to the standards set by the International Association of Lighthouse Authorities (IALA). These regulations include the standard of red buoys on the starboard side and green port-side buoys along with orange-and-white-striped safe-water buoys. In addition, red buoys (which typically have red lights) are assigned even numbers and green buoys (usually with green lights) are given odd numbers that increase as a vessel approaches a port.

The Intracoastal Waterway

Buoys play a significant role in the orderly trips that occur every day in the Intracoastal Waterway (ICW). The Intracoastal Waterway is a recreational and commercial watercourse that extends about 3,000 miles (4,830 kilometers) along the Atlantic and Gulf coasts of the United States, making it possible for boats to travel along inland channels without having to go far offshore. The ICW runs from Manasquan Inlet, New Jersey, to Key West, Florida, and then from the Saint Mark's River in northern Florida to the Texas-Mexico border.

With human-made canals, sheltered bays, barrier islands, and natural river channels, the different sections of the ICW offer plenty of safe harbors for vessels of all types and sizes. However, setting a course along the ICW should only be attempted by those experienced in open-water navigation. A solid knowledge of navigation, right-of-way, and markers is important.

Along the Intracoastal Waterway, and the U.S. Atlantic coast in general, red buoys are always placed on the right or shore side when a vessel is traveling south along the East coast. The same is true when heading north in the Pacific toward Alaska along the West coast.

A UNIQUE HABITAT, WETLANDS SURROUND THE INTRACOASTAL WATERWAY AS IT WINDS ALONG THE GULF OF MEXICO IN NORTHERN COASTAL TEXAS.

THE REDUCED VISIBILITY OF DUSK MEANS A WORKING SET OF LIGHTS IS ESSENTIAL.

Buoys and the lights of beacons and lighthouses are helpful guides along coasts and in harbors and ports. However, a sailor cannot rely on them alone. Floating navigational aids may not always be at their expected positions or they may not always be functioning as they are supposed to. Careful sailors consult a chart to verify the position of the channel and of shoals and other obstacles.

Navigational Lights

Having green lights on the port side and red on the starboard side applies as well to side lights, signals that are found on the sides of vessels. Navigational lights on a ship help to make the vessel visible to other ships both at night and in bad weather. The colors and the placement of the navigational lights show the ship's orientation in the water or the direction in which it is traveling and well as its size and type.

The colors used (including white, red, green, yellow, and blue), the prescribed range of visibility (how far away a boat's lights are able to be seen), and the position of the lights are determined by national and international regulations. Every captain is legally responsible for displaying lights of the correct color, intensity, location, and visibility on the boat. Sailors must be able to interpret the lights displayed by other vessels so they can gauge the course and position of another vessel and, as required by safety rules, know when to yield the right-of-way to an oncoming or passing vessel.

For centuries, navigators sailing on the water's surface struggled to use objects and points of reference they could see in order to accurately determine their position or direction. Underwater navigation, with vessels locked in the depths of the ocean, presented a new set of challenges.

Navigation by Radio and Sound Waves

Imagine the world of the future. Everyone carries a data chip that records their exact destination whether they travel by automobile, ship, or airplane. No more tickets to remember or worries about getting lost. Modern technology promises to make travel effortless and foolproof. These technologies that assist navigation use, among other things, sound and radio waves, precise timekeeping, and the benefits of the computer age.

Undersea Navigation

The submarine warfare of World War I prompted the British to invent a system using sound waves and their echoes to detect the underwater vessels. This system is now known as sonar, which stands for *so*und *na*vigation and *r*anging. Sonar determines underwater distances by bouncing sound waves off objects and then measuring the time it takes for the echoes to come back. Sonar, which imitates the way dolphins and whales navigate, is also used by ships to check the ocean depth and to detect the presence of deep ocean currents, schools of fish, shipwrecks, and submarines.

Sonar systems contain components that allow them to send and receive sound waves. These include an acoustic (sound) pulse generator, a transducer that produces sound waves in a narrow beam, amplifiers that increase the sound intensity, a sound detector, a delay timer, and an electronic display. The display shows the topography or surface of the seafloor in front of or below a ship. The distance to an object or a change in the terrain is indicated by the time it takes for the echo to return.

Depth Finders

Depth finders are as important to fishermen as to submarine crews. The devices work on any body of water and at great depths. A depth finder works by measuring the time it takes for an ultrasonic energy pulse—with a frequency higher than the human ear can detect—to travel from the instrument to the bottom and then back up to the instrument. Depth finders are valuable tools as they record the depth of water under a boat, a reading that adjusts as the depth itself increases or decreases. These devices warn seamen of sudden changes in depth that occur over a reef or at the edges of a deep channel.

Radio Directional Finders

There are several radio navigation systems commonly used aboard fishing and pleasure boats as well as on large commercial and military ships. These tools range from simple to complex, depending on the type of receiving equipment required.

One application of radio waves as a navigational aid is the radio direction finder (RDF), a system that employs a directional antenna. The directional antenna, invented in 1916, detects the direction from which a radio signal is transmitted. The radio direction finder was developed by the U.S. Navy during World War I and came into civilian use after the war. Today it is used especially by smaller vessels.

Most RDF systems have several main parts: an actual unit on a boat, radio transmitters onshore, and charts covering the transmitters' locations and areas of operation. An RDF set on a boat includes a radio receiver and a directional antenna, along with an indicator to find the boat's exact position. The transmitter creates radio waves in brief pulses of energy. The directional antenna receives the radio signals and determines where they are coming from. The receiver detects the

HAND-HELD DEPTH FINDERS TAKE SOME OF THE MYSTERY AND GUESSWORK OUT OF FISHING. THE DEVICES NOT ONLY MEASURE THE WATER'S DEPTH, MANY CAN ALSO DETECT THE PRESENCE OF THE ELUSIVE CREATURES SWIMMING BELOW.

THE RED-LIT NAVIGATION ROOM OF A SUBMARINE.

signals, magnifies them, and calculates the ship's position. The indicator displays the ship's location on a computer screen.

LORAN-C

The radio navigation system most often used in U.S. coastal waters is the *long-range navigation* system or LORAN-C. This system is also in use around Canada, northwestern Europe, and parts of Asia. LORAN-C was developed in the United States during World War II. Like finding direction by radio waves, the system uses radio transmitters from three different points onshore and radio receivers on the ship to enable seamen to find their location at sea. The differences in the time it takes for radio signals from the three onshore transmitters to reach the ship's receivers are used to plot the ship's location. LORAN-C uses the precise timekeeping of a cesium clock, a type of atomic clock, and can plot the ship's location to within 164 feet (50 meters).

Satellite navigational aids, such as the global positioning system (GPS), work on the same principle. Once GPS became available, LORAN-C could be seen as an unnecessary duplication. But mariners like the LORAN-C system because the signals are not as easily interfered with as those sent by satellites. As a result, LORAN-C location readings are more dependable. Some sailors use both LORAN-C and GPS as a means to not only verify that the two systems are working properly but to give them a true reading of the ship's position as well.

A MAN USES HIS GLOBAL POSITIONING DEVICE TO AID HIM ON A TREK OFF THE BEATEN PATH. WITH THE ONSET OF NEW TECHNOLOGY OFFERING ACCURATE LOCATION INFORMATION, GETTING LOST MAY BECOME A CHALLENGE.

Navigation by Satellite

The future will reveal even more sophisticated navigational technology. For now, the development of the global positioning system (GPS) has caused its own revolution in personal navigational aids. Many luxury cars are now available with navigation systems that include a GPS receiver that can display the car's location on a digital map. Hand-held GPS navigation units are available that pinpoint a position (latitude, longitude, and altitude) from within 16 to 33 feet (5 to 10 meters). Mariners have found the GPS to be an invaluable aid to navigation on the seas.

GPS consists of twenty-four satellites orbiting approximately 11,000 miles (17,710 kilometers) above the Earth and the ground stations that monitor them and the signals they emit. Each GPS satellite has a computer, an atomic clock accurate to one nanosecond or one-billionth of a second, and a radio that is constantly communicating the satellite's position and the time. GPS satellites are positioned so that from any point on Earth, four satellites are above the horizon and visible from any point at any given time. Users on Earth pick up the signals through a receiver and can determine their longitude, latitude, altitude, speed, and the time. The GPS receiver is able to provide this information by comparing the time signals it receives from three or four satellites. From the differences, it calculates the user's position.

GPS and Time

GPS was created by the U.S. Department of Defense while conducting military navigational research. It was designed to provide a satellite-based navigation system for military operations. Today GPS meets both military and civilian navigation needs. The first of the GPS satellites was launched in 1978, but the basic technology that makes GPS possible was developed before World War II.

Scientists discovered high-precision techniques that allowed them to figure out the details of atomic structure and build an atomic clock. They based their work on Albert Einstein's theory of gravity and time, which states that gravity is distorted by time and space. A clock on Mount Everest, for example, will run thirty-millionths of a second faster per day than the identical clock at sea level. The only way to test the prediction of these time differences was to use a much more accurate clock capable of measuring smaller increments of time.

The development of quartz clocks marked an improvement. The vibrations of a quartz crystal can be measured to an accuracy of less than one-thousandth of a second per day. However, to prove the theory of gravity, devices were needed that were even more accurate and able to measure smaller amounts of time.

A major leap forward came in the 1930s when I. I. Rabi, a researcher at Columbia University, invented a technique called magnetic resonance to study the properties of atoms and their nuclei or centers. Rabi noticed that each individual atom gives off an electromagnetic wave of energy of a specific frequency, similar to how different radio stations transmit their signals at different frequencies. When Rabi discovered that the atoms of each element had their own unique frequency, he wondered if atoms could be used to make a clock of extreme accuracy. For his efforts, Rabi was awarded the Nobel Prize for Physics in 1944.

In 1954 a colleague of Rabi's, Jerrold Zacharias from the Massachusetts Institute of Technology (MIT), joined the National Company and in 1956 produced the first commercial atomic clock, which was called the atomichron.

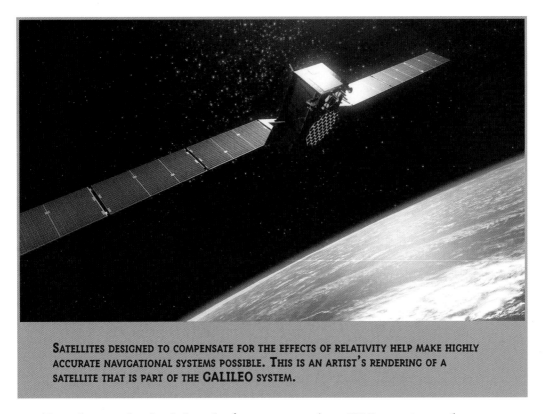

SATELLITES DESIGNED TO COMPENSATE FOR THE EFFECTS OF RELATIVITY HELP MAKE HIGHLY ACCURATE NAVIGATIONAL SYSTEMS POSSIBLE. THIS IS AN ARTIST'S RENDERING OF A SATELLITE THAT IS PART OF THE GALILEO SYSTEM.

To achieve the high level of precision that GPS requires, the amount of time it takes for the signals from four satellites to reach a GPS receiver must be accurate up to twenty to thirty nanoseconds. The motion of the satellites relative to the Earth has a minor effect on those times, which must be taken into account. Otherwise, too many fluctuations in timekeeping would enter the system, making it inexact and useless as a tool for finding location.

The engineers who designed the GPS system made allowances for this time-motion discrepancy and designed the satellite system to compensate for the effects of relativity (the faster something is traveling, the slower its time). Additionally, GPS receivers have built-in computers that make needed corrections when calculating location.

The cesium atomic clocks used in GPS are all based on the atomichron. Most atomic clocks today are accurate to within 1 second in 100,000 years. The United States's atomic clock, which sets the time standard at the National Institute of Standards and Technology, has an estimated accuracy of 1 second in 3 million years.

These highly accurate ways of measuring time have helped to advance navigation. Atomic clocks have been used in satellites, automobiles, and ground-control systems.

Many other advances contributed to the development of GPS as well. Besides radio navigation, these include satellite launching and control methods, microchips, advanced circuitry, and microwave communication.

Uses of GPS

GPS is used in a wide variety of ways. Receivers have map displays showing individual locations, and some systems use verbal directional instructions as well to help drivers find their destinations.

GPS is used by a range of occupations. Emergency vehicles rely on GPS to find their way and to map routes. Trucking and transportation companies track deliveries; shipping companies monitor and control the movement of fleets using GPS. Pleasure boats and military ships depend on the technology for accurate navigation. Private aircraft pilots utilize GPS for navigation, crop dusting, surveying, and aerial photography. Major airlines rely on its precise instrument guidance and tracking. Telecommunications companies synchronize their land-based digital networks via GPS, making sure their systems all keep the same timing. Scientists also rely on the technology to advance their knowledge of forest fires, hurricanes, and earthquakes.

When the twenty-fourth satellite was launched on March 9, 1994, it completed a communications network that provides twenty-four hours of service, seven days a week, making it available to a wide range of users. One possible drawback of this increased exposure and availability has been the concern that it may be used by thieves, terrorists, or other hostile forces.

To address this concern, in the past the U.S. military established a policy known as selective availability, in which the most accurate GPS signals transmitted were reserved strictly for military and other approved users. For example, GPS satellites currently send out two signals: one for public use accurate to about 40 feet (12 meters) and a second signal accurate to a few inches or centimeters that could be decoded only by military equipment. Additionally, the military was granted the ability to purposely introduce errors at any time, as in during a national security threat, that make the publicly available signals much less accurate. This policy of selective availability was discontinued in 2000 by President Clinton. The U.S government is committed to increasing GPS accuracy for peaceful public, commercial, and scientific use around the world.

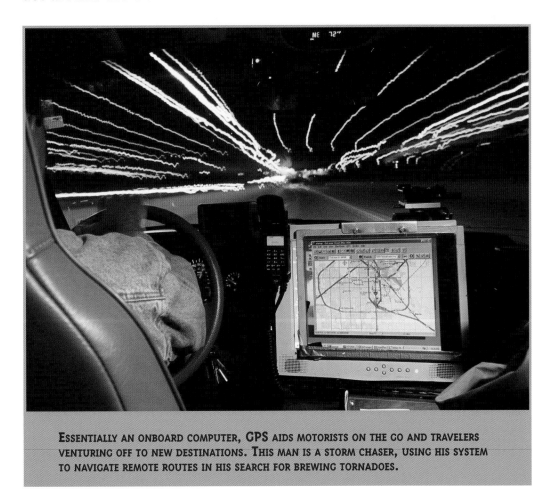

ESSENTIALLY AN ONBOARD COMPUTER, GPS AIDS MOTORISTS ON THE GO AND TRAVELERS VENTURING OFF TO NEW DESTINATIONS. THIS MAN IS A STORM CHASER, USING HIS SYSTEM TO NAVIGATE REMOTE ROUTES IN HIS SEARCH FOR BREWING TORNADOES.

DGPS

The U.S. Coast Guard (USCG) maritime differential GPS (DGPS) helps increase the accuracy and availability of the global positioning system. The U.S. Coast Guard Navigation Center in Alexandria, Virginia, controls and operates more than sixty land-based transmitting sites. In addition to the GPS signal, DGPS sends out corrected GPS information on a medium-frequency radio signal, the range used by mariners. DGPS alerts mariners to GPS errors. Planning for DGPS began in 1979, soon after the first GPS satellite was launched, and the system became operational in 1999.

Combined GPS and DGPS receivers are accurate from within 10 feet (3 meters) to 30 feet (9 meters). The system serves the coastal waters, the Great Lakes, Hawaii, parts of Alaska, and the waterways of the Mississippi river basin. To provide this service to the remote parts of the United States, the USCG teams up with the U.S. Army Corps of Engineers. Together they operate twenty receiving sites along rivers in the western United States. All these receiving stations utilize National Oceanic and Atmospheric Administration equipment for exact positioning and surveying.

By adding more public frequencies, signal towers and satellite services are more easily updated. This improves satellite dependability and protects against possible interference from the ionosphere or terrorists. Coordination of international rescue operations, water navigation, and flight control is also easier and more accurate.

GALILEO

Satellite radio navigation uses signals that provide extremely precise time measurements. In this way, the position of an individual or an object—such as a car or a ship—can be determined to within a few feet using a small receiver. GPS is only one of these systems; other space agencies have developed similar satellite-navigation systems.

GALILEO, a project of the European Commission and the European Space Agency, is Europe's contribution to global satellite navigation.

A RUSSIAN SOYUZ ROCKET CARRYING A GIOVE-A SATELLITE, PART OF GALILEO'S GLOBAL POSITIONING SYSTEM, BLASTS OFF ON DECEMBER 28, 2005.

The first GALILEO satellite was launched on December 28, 2005.

When complete, GALILEO will support thirty satellites and several ground stations and provide information on the location of nearly anything with a receiver. The system will be useful for transportation systems, social services, police operations, and emergency services, as well as for recreational activities such as boating and hiking. The GALILEO project is expected to more than double the United States's GPS coverage and provide satellite-navigation access to everyone.

GALILEO gets its high degree of precision from two onboard atomic clocks—the passive hydrogen maser (microwave-signal) clock and the rubidium atomic frequency clock. These clocks, which measure time for the newest navigational satellites, record atomic vibrations to an accuracy of more than one-billionth of a second per hour. With the clocks working together, GALILEO's navigational signals are transmitted through a signal generator, antenna, and related equipment.

Precise time signals travel at the speed of light, reporting fractions of a second with great accuracy. The precision of the atomic clocks is key to finding specific locations anywhere on the Earth's surface to within 18 inches (46 centimeters).

GLONASS

The Russian Federation also has a satellite-based navigation system, called GLONASS, similar to GPS and GALILEO. The first GLONASS satellite was launched in December 1983. Later, more satellites were sent into orbit to complete the system and then to replace aging satellites as they were taken out of service. The system went into operation in December 1995. When complete, the network will have twenty-four satellites in orbit at about 11,800 miles (19,000 kilometers) above the Earth.

Global Importance

Navigation system receivers are employed by craft that are mid-ocean or far from a landmass, since signals provide position as well as vessel identification. This allows for better control of oceangoing

TWO TECHNICIANS PUT THE FINISHING TOUCHES ON THE LATEST RUSSIAN GLONASS SATELLITE TO BE SENT INTO ORBIT.

traffic, increases safety, and prevents collisions. Although midocean collisions are not common, many have been recorded over the past two hundred years.

Since most watches or onboard guard duty in the past were overseen by young seamen perched atop the mast in the crow's nest, it is not hard to imagine the opportunities for error. An inexperienced sailor, thick fog, no moon, and heavily traveled coastal sea routes were often the occasion for bringing ships within close range of each other.

Satellite navigation has applications in marine surveying, dredging, and maintaining harbors and waterways. Today's map makers and engineers require exact positioning to locate underwater obstacles, lay cable and pipelines, and find deep-drilling oil platforms. Fishermen find satellite-navigation systems helpful in locating lobster traps and fishing nets and in monitoring fishing boats when they travel as a group. Satellite-based navigational aids are useful in tracking the movement of shipping containers and in the automatic piloting of barges.

Satellite-navigation networks also provide an important tool for environmental studies that depend on data collected by monitoring things like sea levels, tides, and currents. In projects such as these, buoys in the study area relay their positional data to satellites. Scientists then combine the data with Earth-based observation and remote sensing information to see what the various results reveal about the oceans and the global ecosystem.

Satellite networks help with all kinds of nautical maneuvering in many different weather scenarios. Even experienced captains who have sailed into a given port hundreds of times use these modern aids when rough conditions threaten to smash them against rocks or while entering or leaving even the most familiar harbors in uncertain or low-visibility conditions.

Sailors find satellite navigation useful when traveling inland waterways as well. Along narrow rivers and canals where expert navigation is critical to safety, GPS and other systems have made navigation much easier for novice sailors as well as experienced seamen. This same

Thar She Blows!

Rocky shores and oncoming vessels are not the only objects a sailor must be careful to avoid. The migration paths of many whale species cross the world's busy shipping lanes. For one species—the endangered North Atlantic right whale—that migrates along the Atlantic coast of the United States, collisions with ships are a leading cause of death.

Today the population of the North Atlantic right whale is about three hundred. To prevent or at least reduce the number of collisions and to protect the right whale population, several regulations have been adopted or proposed since 1997. These rules, for example, require a ship to maintain a certain distance from the whales and to report the sightings to the U.S. Coast Guard so that other ships in the area can be alerted to their presence. The National Oceanic and Atmospheric Administration has established sea routes that go around the whales during migration to reduce the likelihood of collisions. It has also proposed that ships travel at slow speeds when crossing areas where the whales are likely to be present. Satellite-navigational aids can warn ships if whales are in the vicinity and help in the efforts to prevent their extinction.

technology has vastly improved search-and-rescue response times. Satellite navigation allows officers to pinpoint the location of the distress call to within a few feet. In this way, rescue centers can respond faster to people in danger, thus saving more lives.

Navigational Software

Navigational programs are available for personal and hand-held computers too. These programs feature high-speed graphics and a wide variety of chart formats. For commercial seamen, the software is compatible with digital charts, their own charts that they scan in, and U.S. Geological Survey topographical maps. The navigational programs have many applications, although several have been specifically designed for marine navigation. Many programs work with GPS units too.

Unlike the danger and uncertainty faced by many seamen in past centuries, navigating the world's waters to-day is a lot like playing a video game on a computer screen. Gone are the days of leaving family and friends to explore uncharted waters with a good chance of never returning. With satellite navigation and positioning networks, knowledgeable navigators have little reason to become lost.

Navy captains, for example, use satellite guidance to provide direct computer control of a ship's position and track. They need only to program shipboard systems to automatically follow a specific navigational track. Some ships can even be driven from the bridge or operations room with a joystick, just like a video game.

Electronic Aids

With all the advances in electronics in the past few years, navigational aids have been greatly improved. This has given those who enjoy recreational sailing and boating, especially, an increased sense of security. One drawback, though, is that now many inexperienced sailors rely heavily on GPS and other electronic aids. If the sailors become lost or the electronic devices malfunction, they often do not have the nautical skills to figure out their position or heading on their own. As a result, those seamen put themselves and others in danger, especially if a storm whips up.

Some people believe the GPS satellite

IN THE PAST, SAILORS RELIED ON EXPERIENCE, GUESSWORK, AND INACCURATE INFORMATION TO ATTEMPT TO REACH THEIR INTENDED DESTINATIONS. ONCE, A SUCCESSFUL JOURNEY FROM CHILE, WHERE THESE SIGNPOSTS ARE FOUND, TO ANY OF THE FAR-OFF LOCATIONS INDICATED WOULD BE UNTHINKABLE.

network—able to provide longitude and latitude positions for every location on Earth—renders the sextant, magnetic compass, and other devices useless and out of date. But these navigational aids are still useful in emergencies and during a loss of electricity. Experienced captains carry charts and other navigational tools to double-check onboard electronics. Still, technology leads the way in assisting those needing to get safely and efficiently from one point to another.

Whether mariners use navigational instruments that receive and process signals from satellites or radio transmitters or take their readings from an astrolabe, a compass, or a chart, they need these aids for the same purpose: to know their course, speed, position, the locations of safe sea lanes, the coast, and potential hazards up ahead. Mariners, both modern and ancient, have utilized the Earth's elements and natural forces (such as the winds, magnetism, and sound and radio waves) and the paths of heavenly objects

ALTHOUGH NAVIGATIONAL AIDS HAVE GROWN INCREASINGLY SOPHISTICATED AND ACCURATE THROUGH THE CENTURIES, THE SIMPLE DEVICES THAT PAVED THE WAY FOR MORE RECENT BREAKTHROUGHS PROVE JUST AS EFFECTIVE WHEN CONFUSED TRAVELERS ARE FACED WITH THE OFTEN DIFFICULT QUESTION: WHERE ARE WE?

to chart their voyages across the same tumultuous oceans. Since humans first put boats into the water, they have employed ingenuity and a variety of navigational aids to help them arrive safely and directly at their destinations and to return to their home ports. Human life has been enriched by this desire to explore and know new places and other worlds.

Time Line

around 2500 BCE
Egyptian traders reach the island of Crete.

sixth century BCE
The sounding weight is first used.

240 BCE
The world's first lighthouse is constructed in Alexandria, Egypt.

early 200s BCE
The first magnetic compass is developed in China.

around 100 BCE
The Tower of the Winds, a water clock and observatory, is built in Athens, Greece.

1100s CE
The first use of the compass as a navigational aid, by Chinese diplomat Zheng He, is recorded. The instrument is widely used among Chinese sailors.

1200s
The mariner's quadrant is first used.

1400s
The mariner's astrolabe becomes a commonly used navigational device.

1420

A navigation and exploration center is founded in Sagres, Portugal.

1488

Bartolomeu Dias rounds the Cape of Good Hope.

1498

Vasco da Gama completes a sea route to India.

1519–1522

Ferdinand Magellan leads the first expedition to circumnavigate the globe. Although a few surviving crew members complete the journey, Magellan is killed in 1521 in the Philippines.

1590s

English scientist and mariner John Davis develops the back-staff.

1594

English queen Elizabeth I grants the Guild of Shipmen and Mariners the right to install buoys in rivers and sea-lanes.

1600

William Gilbert publishes his treatise on magnetism, *De magnete*.

1716

The first U.S. lighthouse, Boston Light, is built beside the city's harbor.

1730

American mathematician Thomas Godfrey submits his modified quadrant design to England's Royal Society.

1731

The Royal Society publishes its description of John Hadley's sextant.

1745

English inventor Gowin Knight develops a compass with a steel needle that is able to retain magnetization for longer periods than earlier compasses.

1783
Swiss scientist Aimé Argand is the first to use a reflector to intensify a beam of light.

1789
The U.S. Congress establishes federal support for the maintenance of lighthouses, buoys, beacons, and public piers.

1822
The first Fresnel lens is installed, in France's Cardovan Tower.

1848
The U.S. Congress adopts the lateral system for color coding buoys, also known as the "red, right, return" system.

1852
French physicist Jean Bernard Leon Foucault names the gyroscope, which had been developed earlier in the nineteenth century.

1908
German Hermann Anschutz creates the first gyrocompass.

1916
The directional antenna is invented.

1938
Columbia University researcher I. I. Rabi discovers magnetic resonance.

1954
The world's oldest ship is discovered in Egyptian pharaoh Cheops's tomb.

1956
Jerrold Zacharias, working for the National Company, produces the first

commercial atomic clock—the atomichron.

1973
The development of the NAVSTAR global positioning system is approved by the U.S. Department of Defense.

1978
The first NAVSTAR satellite is launched.

1983
The first GLONASS satellite is sent into orbit.

1989–1994
Twenty-three GPS satellites are launched.

1996
The United States announces its aim of providing more accurate global positioning information for all.

2000
The National Institute of Standards puts into use an atomic clock accurate to within one second every three million years.

2005
The first GALILEO satellite is launched.

2010s
The GLONASS and GALILEO satellite systems are slated for completion.

accelerometer—An instrument used to measure acceleration and the effects of gravity.

astrolabe—An ancient astronomical device used to establish the time of day or the time of the sunrise or sunset. Also used to find the positions of planets, constellations, and other heavenly bodies.

back-staff—A navigational instrument used for measuring the altitude of the sun and other celestial bodies and objects. The implement got its name from the position the user assumed, with his or her back turned to the sun.

chronometer—A highly accurate and reliable timepiece.

circumnavigate—To travel completely around an object or place.

compass—A navigational instrument used to find direction. It has a magnetized pointer, usually referred to as a needle, that aligns itself with the Earth's magnetic field.

course—The direction a craft is taking on its path through the water or atmosphere.

cross-staff—A device used for measuring the altitude of a heavenly body. It is made up of the main staff with a sliding crosspiece set at a right angle to it. The end of the main shaft is held to the observer's eye, with the crosspiece positioned to line up with the horizon and the celestial object sighted. The crosspiece marks a specific point on the staff that, with the consultation of a table or chart of degrees and minutes, determines altitude.

dead reckoning—A method for finding a ship's approximate position by using its last position relative to geographic north and the direction in which it is traveling.

declination—The latitude, written in degrees, of a ship, calculated by using the sun's position as it moves north or south of the equator with the seasons.

deviation—The amount of error in a magnetic compass when it is attracted to nearby metals as well as to magnetic north.

diffraction—Dispersal; the bending and redirection of light waves.

flotsam—Debris floating in the water such as wood, glass, buoys, or other objects carried away from their original locations by ocean currents and the motion of the waves.

global positioning system (GPS)—A series of 24 NAVSTAR satellites, located in precise orbits approximately 12,000 miles (19,320 kilometers) above the Earth, that provide signals that are then analyzed by ground GPS receivers to compute position, speed, and time.

heading—The horizontal direction that a ship is pointing at a specific instant—measured in degrees clockwise from 0 degrees to 359 degrees—from a reference point such as geographic north.

horizon—The horizontal line of sight where the Earth meets the sky.

Intracoastal Waterway (ICW)—A system of rivers and canals along the Atlantic and Gulf coasts of the United States that allows ships to travel along its course without having to head offshore.

kamal—An early Arabic device, made of wood and knotted string, that was used to find latitude by holding the wood between the horizon and the North Star.

latitude—The distance of a point on the Earth's surface north or south of the equator. The equator is latitude 0 degrees. The North Pole is latitude 90 degrees north, and the South Pole is latitude 90 degrees south.

longitude—The distance of a point on the Earth's surface east or west from an imaginary line that runs through Greenwich, England, and cuts the globe into western and eastern halves. Greenwich is longitude 0 degrees. Places west of Greenwich have positive (+) longitudes; places east of Greenwich have negative (–) longitudes.

LORAN—An acronym that stands for *long-range navigation*. An electronic system using shore-based radio transmitters and shipboard receivers to establish positions in the water.

magnetic resonance—The absorption of electromagnetic radiation of a specific frequency by an atomic nucleus.

magnetite—A black mineral form of iron oxide, one of the major ores found in iron. Ancient navigators used one strongly magnetic variety, lodestone, in early compasses.

navigation—The process of accurately determining a certain course or direction to reach a desired destination.

quadrant—A hand-held device used to find altitude that looks like a quarter of a circle. Ninety degrees are marked along its curved edge and a plumb bob or weight hangs from its upper corner.

sextant—A hand-held navigational instrument that measures the altitude, or angle above the horizon, of any celestial body.

sonar—An acronym derived from the phrase *sound navigation and ranging*; a system that establishes distance underwater by bouncing sound waves off other objects and measuring the time it takes for the signals to return.

sounding—Measuring how deep water is, usually with the help of a rope with a lead weight tied to its end.

topography—The shape of the Earth's surface both above and below the oceans.

track—Also referred to as intended track, the path a ship's captain plans to take.

Web Sites

Astrolabe
http://www.astrolabes.org

Charting Neptune's Realm
http://usm.maine.edu/maps/exhibit8/nrintro.html

The Columbus Navigation Home Page
http://www.columbusnavigation.com

Determination of Latitude by Francis Drake on the
Coast of California in 1579
http://www.longcamp.com/nav.html

Exploration through the Ages
http://www.mariner.org/exploration/index.php

Geomagnetism
http://gsc.nrcan.gc.ca/geomag/nmp/early_nmp_e.php

Global Positioning System
http://ec.europa.eu/dgs/energy_transport/galileo/index_en.htm

History of Navigation
http://www.boatsafe.com/kids/navigation.htm

Lighthouses
http://www.pbs.org/legendarylighthouses/
http://www.uscg.mil/hq/g-cp/history/h_lighthousefacts.html

The Longitude Problem
http://www.nmm.ac.uk/server/show/conWebDoc.355/viewPage1

Marine Navigation in the Age of Exploration
http://www.seattleartmuseum.org/exhibit/interactives/spain/
launchWin.htm

Bibliography

Books

FOR STUDENTS
Gurney, Alan. *Compass: A Story of Exploration and Innovation.* New York: W. W. Norton, 2004.

Pike, Dag. *Reed's Sextant Simplified.* Dobbs Ferry, NY: Sheridan House, 2003.

Shufeldt, H. H. *Piloting and Dead Reckoning.* Annapolis, MD: Naval Institute Press, 1999.

Sobel, Dava. *Longitude: The True Story of a Lone Genius Who Solved the Greatest Scientific Problem of His Time.* New York: Walker, 1995.

FOR TEACHERS OR ADVANCED READERS
Bauer, Bruce. *The Sextant Handbook.* 2nd ed. New York: McGraw-Hill, 1995.

Egbert, Robert I., and Joseph E. King. *The GPS Handbook.* Short Hills, NJ: Burford Books, 2003.

Maloney, Elbert S. *Chapman Piloting and Seamanship*. New York: Hearst Books, 2006.

Rousmaniere, John. *The Annapolis Book of Seamanship*. New York: Simon & Schuster, 1999.

Stapleton, Sid. *Stapleton's Powerboat Bible: The Complete Guide to Selection, Seamanship, and Cruising*. Camden, ME: International Marine/McGraw-Hill, 2002.

Sweet, Robert. *The Weekend Navigator: Simple Boat Navigation with GPS and Electronics*. Camden, ME: International Marine/McGraw-Hill, 2005.

Index

Page numbers in **boldface** are illustrations.

About the Author

Linda Williams is a nonfiction writer with specialties in science, medicine, and space. Williams's experience has ranged from biochemistry and microbiology to genetics and human enzyme research. Formerly, Williams was a lead scientist and technical writer for NASA and McDonnell Douglas Space Systems, and a science speaker for the Medical Sciences Division at NASA-Johnson Space Center in Houston. She is the founder of the Science Cafe–Little Rock, a public venue for the discussion of scientific topics. Williams now works at the University of Arkansas for the Medical Sciences, Little Rock, Arkansas. This is her first book for Marshall Cavendish Benchmark.